Zodiac MOSAIC CROCHET

A celestial guide to overlay colorwork

Alexis Sixel

DAVID & CHARLES
— PUBLISHING —

www.davidandcharles.com

TABLE OF CONTENTS

INTRODUCTION

Get ready to take your hook on an astrological journey through the galaxy! I have been dreaming about designing zodiac mosaic crochet patterns for a long time, but I wanted to create a collection of all of them together, so the idea of a book was born.

This book contains mosaic crochet charts for all 12 zodiac signs, with 10 different projects that you can customize with any sign or glyph you choose, and a round blanket pattern that pulls everything together. And it has lots and lots of stars for crocheting yourself into a celestial haven!

Although I'm not an expert in astrology, writing this book gave me the opportunity to do a deep dive into all the zodiac signs and learn more about how all the signs influence each other and how we interact with the world around us. We love watching documentaries at our house, and my new favorite hobby has become trying to guess which zodiac sign celebrities are, based on their personalities and all the drama that surrounds them. It's really fascinating how some people are stereotypically their sign, and others will surprise you with a twist you didn't expect.

Of course we don't always fit perfectly into our stereotypical zodiac traits. We are all multifaceted and there are a lot of factors that influence our personalities. The time and place of our birth also determines our moon and rising signs, which represent our emotions and personality traits. And it takes time to grow into our signs, because as kids we aren't faced with the same obstacles we have as mature adults, so our zodiac traits haven't had time to fully engage.

Regardless of how into astrology you are, I hope you'll find the projects and designs in this book inspiring and fun to crochet.

All of the patterns in the following pages are arranged from easy to advanced. The Glyph project section has smaller and repeatable patterns, while the Zodiac project section features the larger designs and bigger items. And finally we have a round zodiac blanket that uses all of the charts in the book to create a dynamic celestial masterpiece.

You don't need to be a crochet expert to crochet the patterns in this book. All you need is basic crochet knowledge including chains, slip stitches, and single and double crochet stitches. The beginner tutorial and stitch guide at the back of the book will help you learn all the mosaic crochet stitches used to make all of the patterns in this book.

I hope you find this book entertaining and I can't wait to see the hundreds of different combinations of signs and projects everyone crochets!

TOOLS & MATERIALS

Mosaic crochet does not require a lot of tools, just standard crochet hooks, a good pair of small scissors, and a blunt-tip tapestry needle. A full list of any additional tools you'll need will be given for each project.

CROCHET HOOKS

You can use any type of crochet hook you like, but be sure to choose a hook that has a straight shaft. This will help to keep all of your stitches consistent in size. US hook sizes are given as a letter and number, and European sizes are in millimeters – each pattern gives the hook size in both ways.

YARN

All of the yarn used in this book is from Berroco, which is one of my go-to yarn brands for mosaic crochet. It is perfectly fine to substitute any of the yarn in this book, and get creative with different fibers and textures. Some patterns require a certain gauge in order for the project to fit correctly, so as long as you're within the same gauge as the project, it's OK to use whatever yarn you like.

STITCH MARKERS

These are used heavily throughout this book to mark different zodiac signs, and to use as a guide for counting stitches. I recommend getting 12 different color stitch markers, one to represent each zodiac sign. You can use the power colors for each marker, or assign colors for what you have on hand.

BLOCKING TOOLS

For flat projects like placemats and wall hangings that require flat, straight edges and corners, I recommend using interlocking foam blocking mats with a grid, and rust-proof pins. You can use a spray bottle with water or a steamer to relax the stitches. See **Finishing Techniques: Blocking**.

TAPESTRY NEEDLE

The blunt tip allows this to slide easily between strands to avoid splitting the yarn. You'll only need this for projects that require weaving in tail ends.

GAUGE & SIZING

To ensure a proper fit, it's most important to stay within the pattern gauge (tension) on projects like wearable items, or things that need to fit a certain sized object

Gauge is generally determined by the number of stitches and rows in a square that is 4 inches, or 10 centimeters, but with the projects in this book it's less important to count the number of rows you have in 4in (10cm), because each row is a SC row on the back, and all of the stitches end up measuring close to square. Your gauge swatch should be made using the yarn you'd like to use for your project.

To make your gauge swatch, use the Cross Star Chart and instructions in **Mosaic Crochet Basics: Reading Charts**. To calculate your foundation chain, start with the number of stitches across the chart (7) multiplied by the number of stars across (3), plus 2 for the border stitches: (7 x 3) + 2 = 23.

Note: *if you're using a light worsted (DK) weight yarn or thinner, you may want to make four stars across instead to ensure that your swatch is at least 5in (12.5cm) wide.*

Begin your foundation chain in color A (background color) with 23 chains.

Work the Foundation Rows and border stitches as explained in Mosaic Crochet Basics.

For Rows 1 and 2 follow the instructions in **Mosaic Crochet Basics: Reading Charts**, but remember to add a border stitch at either end of each row and to repeat the chart three times instead of only once.

Rows 3–5: Work the border stitch then work across all 7 stitches of the chart three times to the end of the row, and end with the border stitch.

Row 6: Work a row of SC in the background color, then fasten off.

Turn your swatch over and, using a ruler, count the number of stitches across any of the rows in the middle within 4in (10 cm).

Check the gauge listed in the pattern and compare it to the number of stitches you have. If you have fewer stitches, you'll need to either go down a hook size, crochet tighter, switch to a thinner yarn, or all three. If you have more stitches, you'll need to either go up a hook size, crochet looser, switch to thicker yarn, or all three.

TIP

We have used imperial measurements throughout this book, and the metric conversions provided have been rounded to the nearest 0.5cm. If you need more exact measurements, please use an online converter.

MOSAIC CROCHET BASICS

Mosaic crochet is an exciting colorwork technique that allows you to crochet intricate patterns with fine details easily. Most colorwork techniques involve switching back and forth between different colors in the same row in order to create the design, but with mosaic crochet you're only using one color per row, and the overlay stitches are what create the design in the row below. With this technique you can focus on the different stitches and forget about switching colors.

Mosaic patterns are created by working all SC (single crochet) stitches into the back-loops-only of the top row, and dropping down all DC (overlay double crochet) stitches into the front loops of the row below of the same color. The DC stitches will cover the SC stitches from the previous row. There are also special overlay stitches that are used to create different angles and curves beyond the basic DC stitches. See **Stitches & Techniques: Special Stitches** for instructions.

All projects are worked from the front side only, and charts are read from right to left (or from left to right for left-handed crocheters). Each row alternates between two contrasting colors, color A (background) and color B (design). When following a mosaic crochet chart, the numbered columns on the right and left sides are color coded with the color you will be crocheting the entire row with, either color A or B. The chart we are using for the tutorial (see **Reading Charts: Cross Star Chart**) starts with color A for Row 1 (purple), and color B (white) for Row 2.

All of the patterns in this book are chart based, and are read stitch by stitch in the same direction as you're crocheting. Each box represents one stitch. Once you become familiar with how to read charts it becomes much easier than reading a written pattern because you'll have a visual reference for how each row should look, and where all the stitches will line up in each row.

There are three different mosaic crochet construction techniques used in this book: flat with border stitches; in the round; and flat circles in the round. This beginner tutorial will start with the basics using border stitches, and will continue to instructions for joining projects in the round. All of the flat circle projects are joined in the round and follow the same set of instructions as the blanket pattern (see **Astrology Wheel Blanket** project).

STITCH CONVERSIONS

All the patterns in this book use US stitch names. The UK equivalents are given below.

US name	**UK name**
Single crochet (SC)	Double crochet (DC)
Half double crochet (HDC)	Half treble (HTR)
Double crochet (DC)	Treble crochet (TR)
Treble crochet (TR)	Double treble (DTR)

ABBREVIATIONS

Except for the stitches detailed in Stitch Conversions there are no abbreviations in the patterns.

Square brackets are used to indicate a sequence of stitches that is to be repeated.

Foundation rows

The Cross Star Chart (see **Reading Charts**) has 7 stitches across. Start with color A (background color) and chain 7. Then add 2 more chains for the border stitches.

Foundation Row 1: Chain 1 and SC into the second chain from the hook. SC the entire row to the end. Chain 1, pull down to tighten, cut a 3in (7.5cm) tail and pull through. You will have the same number of stitches in every row as the foundation chain (multiples of 7 plus 2) (**A**).

Foundation Row 2: Start with color B (design color) and add a row of SCs (working in back loops only), starting and ending with a border stitch.

Border stitches

To make a border stitch at the beginning of a row, make a slip knot on your hook with your next color. Add 1 SC into both loops of the first stitch of the row (**B**). Pull down to tighten slightly (**C**).

Continue across the row adding SCs in the back loops up to the last stitch (**D**).

To add a border stitch at the end of the row, add 1 SC into both loops of the last stitch. Pull down to tighten. Chain 1, pull down to tighten, cut a 3in (7.5cm) tail and pull through (**E**).

All remaining rows will start and end with a border stitch into both loops of the previous border stitch.

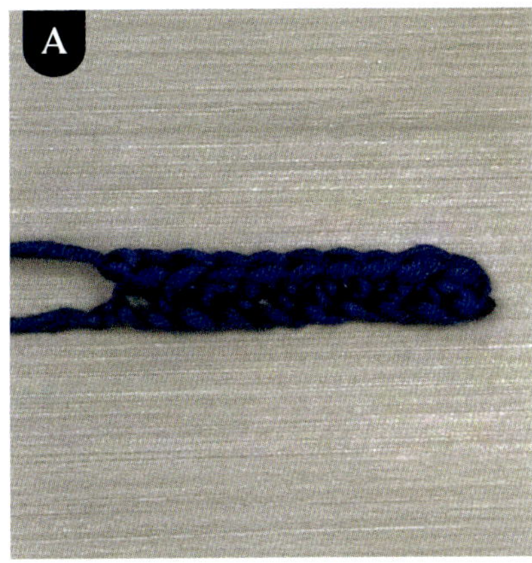

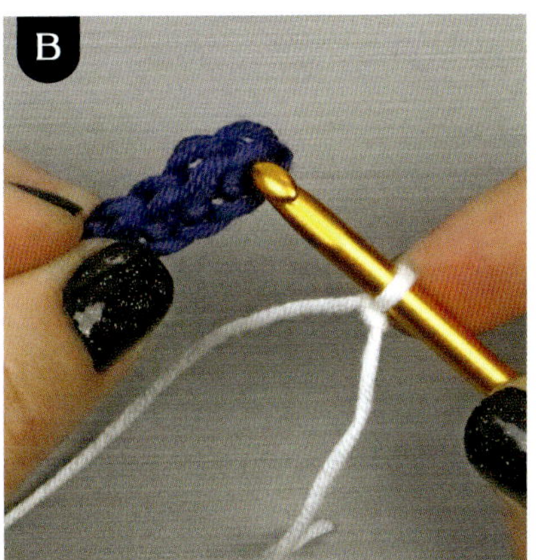

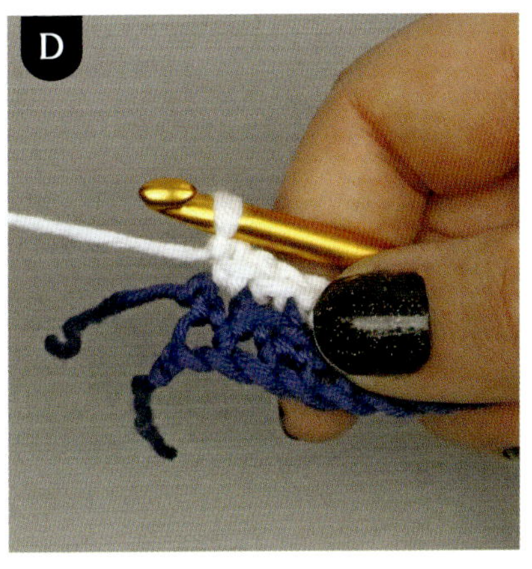

Reading charts

Always start a row with the color indicated in the numbered column of the chart, not the shaded boxes shown in the middle of the chart. Those shaded boxes show you what the row below will look like after you've added overlay stitches to it. Some charts in this book will have entire rows shaded in the opposite color, and that just means there are no overlay stitches in that row.

Looking at the chart, you will be reading each row from right to left (left-handed crocheters will read the chart from left to right). Each box represents one stitch. All DC stitches are marked with an "X" and all SC stitches are blank.

Note: The chart and the following instructions do not include the border stitch that you will work at either end of each row.

CROSS STAR CHART

7 stitches across

5	X	X	X		X	X	X	5
4				X				4
3	X	X				X	X	3
2				X				2
1	X	X	X		X	X	X	1

STITCH KEY

	Single Crochet	All blank boxes SC, top back loop only
X	Double Crochet	DC in the row below of the same color

Chart row 1: The first 3 stitches are DCs (3 Xs). All DCs will be overlay stitches placed in the **front loops of the row below of the same color**. The arrow points to your first DC (**F**). Add 2 more DCs in the next 2 stitches.

The 4th stitch in the row is 1 SC (blank box). All SCs will be placed in the **back loops only** of the top row. The arrow points to your first SC (**G**).

The next 3 stitches are DCs. Add 3 more DCs into the next 3 stitches. The arrow points to your next DC (**H**). Repeat all 7 stitches in the row three times in total. Add a border stitch to finish the row (**I**).

Chart row 2: 3 SCs, 1 DC, 3 SCs. The white DC stitch is placed into the white SC stitch below the blue row (**J**).

Chart row 3: 2 DCs, 3 SCs, 2 DCs (**K**).

Chart row 4: 3 SCs, 1 DC, 3 SCs (**L**).

Chart row 5: 3 DCs, 1 SC, 3 DCs (**M**).

Row 1 Cross Star Chart complete

Row 2 Cross Star Chart complete

Row 3 Cross Star Chart complete

Row 4 Cross Star Chart complete

Row 5 Cross Star Chart complete

Back view of swatch

TIP

When crocheting DCs, the SC stitches from the previous row will be skipped. This will sometimes cause a little pocket to form in the back. This is normal, and once you have several rows it will be less noticeable and even out.

WORKING IN THE ROUND

In the round from foundation row

1. Begin by crocheting a foundation chain and SC row using the number of stitches indicated for your specific project. Wrap the beginning of the row around to meet the end of the row, making sure all of the stitches are facing out and there are no twists in the row (**A**). Connect the bottom of both sides together with a stitch marker or pin to hold the round in place.

2 Pull your hook to make a wider loop, and take out your hook. Insert your hook from the back to the front, through both loops of the first stitch in the round, as shown by the arrow (**B**).

3 Turn your project so you're looking at the back of the round from the inside. It's also easier to insert your hook from this angle. Make sure the working yarn is down towards the inside, and not under your hook on the front side. Hook the open loop (**C**), tighten on your hook and slip stitch to join.

4 With color B, place a slip knot on your hook and slip stitch. Tighten color A. Make sure you don't pull the knot on your hook through the loop. Tighten color B. Chain 1 (**D**). The first stitch for the next round is directly below your hook.

Round 2: All SCs (back loops only) to the end of the round. Join from the back, pull up color A from the back and slip stitch, or join your next color (see step 4). Chain 1. Your first stitch in Round 3 will be directly below your hook.

Round 2 is now complete (**E**). Continue following your pattern, joining and switching colors after each round.

Fasten Off: To end a round after the join, chain 1, tighten, cut a 3–4in (7.5–10cm) tail end and then pull through.

To close the gap at the bottom of the first chain, turn your project over so the bottom is facing up. Using your hook (**F**), weave the tail end through the bottom chains on both sides and pull the tail end through the back.

Both tail ends will now be on the inside of the round. Tie both tail ends together with a square knot to secure (**G**). Weave the tails in along the inside.

In the round from a circle

To join a circle and switch colors, follow the instructions for **In The Round From A Foundation Row** from Step 2.

On the circle, insert your hook from the back into both loops of the top of the first DC as shown (**H, I**). Skip the first 2 chains.

On all remaining rounds, join to the to the top of the first stitch in the round after the first chain.

ZODIAC
Charts

STITCH GUIDE

Here is a guide to the stitch symbols used in the charts. For a full photo tutorial of stitches shown here see the **Stitches & Techniques: Special Stitches** section. If you are left-handed: read the charts from left to right and follow the instructions below backwards.

Symbol	Stitch	Instructions
(blank box)	Single Crochet	All blank boxes SC, top back loop only
X	Double Crochet	DC in the row below of the same color
\ 2	2 DCs	2 DCs, skip the next stitch
2 /	2 DCs	Skip, 2 DCs in next stitch
\ 3 /	3 DCs	Skip, 3 DCs in next stitch, skip next stitch
\ \ 3	3 DCs	3 DCs in next stitch, skip next 2 stitches
3 / /	3 DCs	Skip 2 stitches, 3 DCs in next stitch
(diagonal down symbol)	Diagonal Down	Skip the next stitch, DC, SC above
(diagonal up symbol)	Diagonal Up	SC, DC below, skip the next stitch
(diagonal down) X /	Double Diagonal Down	Skip the next stitch, DC, DC, SC above
\ X (diagonal up)	Double Diagonal Up	SC, DC below, DC, skip the next stitch
D D̄	DC Dec Start SC	SC, 2 DCs decreased below
D̄ D	DC Dec End SC	2 DCs decreased, SC above 2nd DC
D̄ \ D̄	DC Dec Centered	SC, start decrease below, skip, finish decrease, SC above
D̄ D D̄	DC Dec 3 Together	SC, 3 DCs decreased below, SC above 3rd DC
\ ▽ /	Triangle	Skip, DC, SC above, DC below in same stitch, skip

INTRODUCTION TO ASTROLOGY

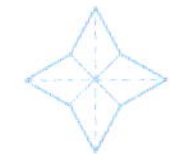

Along with the mosaic crochet charts for each zodiac sign, in this section you'll find a list of personality traits, a description of each zodiac sign, and icons to indicate different glyphs, power colors, elements, zodiac positions, and your constellation in the night sky.

GLYPHS

A glyph is a hieroglyphic symbol that represents each zodiac sign. They share some of the same graphic elements as their zodiac counterpart, and can be used in smaller crochet projects with repeating patterns.

POWER COLORS

Color can have a big impact on your mood and influence many different aspects of your life. Wearing and surrounding yourself with colors that are linked with your zodiac sign can help you feel more empowered, balanced, and more confident being yourself. Warm tones like reds and golds are very lively, and energizing, which is great fit for fire signs and other energetic signs. Cooler tones like blues and greens are more calming and serene, and would feel right at home with a water sign or a sign with deep emotions. Earth tones are very grounding and protective, perfect for earth signs. Purple and pink are great for signs that have a little spunk, creativity, and a bit of romance. You can use the power colors as a guide and inspiration for your own projects or when choosing yarn colors for friends and family. In some projects you'll use colored stitch markers to represent each sign – you can match the markers to the main power colors listed for each sign to help you keep track.

ELEMENTS

The 12 zodiac signs are grouped into four elements, fire, earth, air, and water. These groups of signs share very similar personality traits, aspirations, and outlook on life, and are likely to be more compatible with each other.

- **Fire Signs:** Aries, Leo, Sagittarius (*fiery, dramatic, commanding*)
- **Earth Signs:** Taurus, Virgo, Capricorn (*earthy, grounded, logical*)
- **Air Signs:** Gemini, Libra, Aquarius (*light-hearted, thoughtful, social*)
- **Water Signs:** Cancer, Scorpio, Pisces (*emotional, dreamy, sensitive*)

POSITION

Use these icons as a guide for the position of each zodiac sign around the blanket and wall art patterns. The zodiac wheel shows all of the zodiac signs in order as they appear as constellations in the sky.

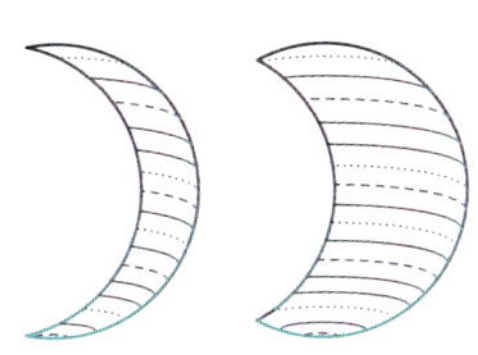

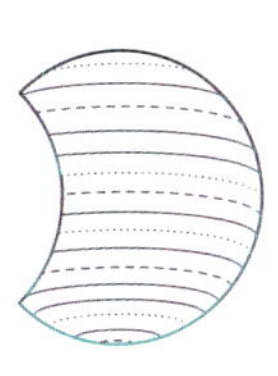

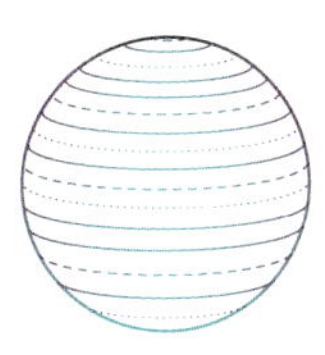

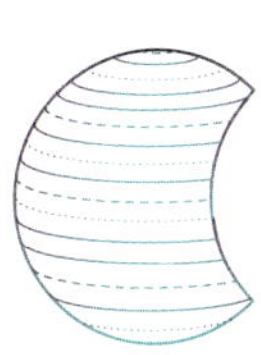

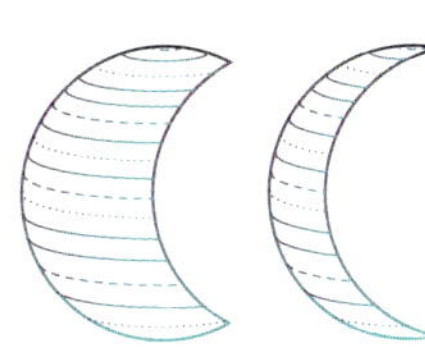

ARIES

March 21 - April 19

Leader | Fiery | Confident

Aries is the first sign of the zodiac and is represented by a ram. People born under this fire sign are born leaders. They are comfortable being first when it comes to trying new things and exploring the world around them. They are strong-willed and passionate about achieving their personal goals. Although Ariens have a bad reputation for being too angsty, this can help spark change.

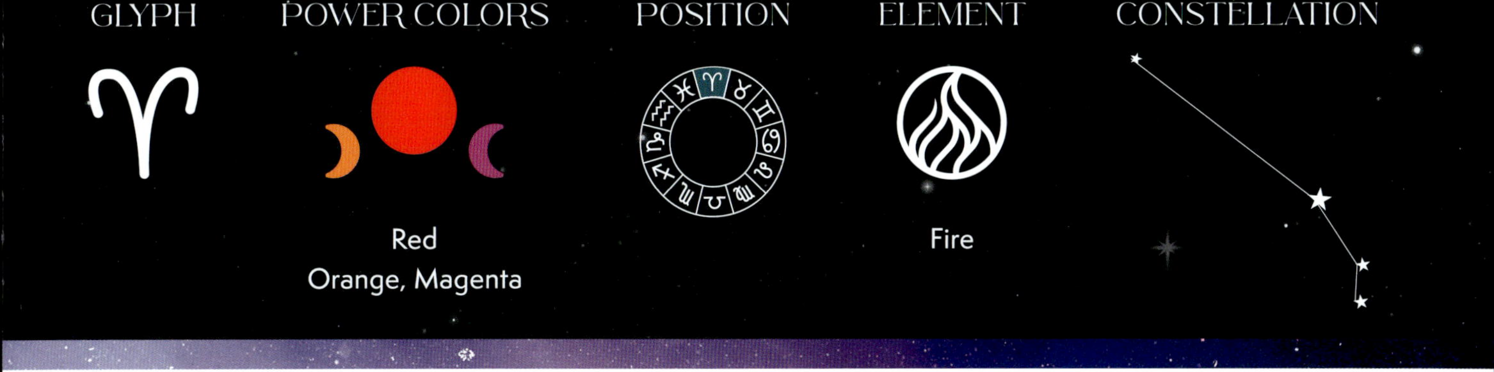

GLYPH | POWER COLORS | POSITION | ELEMENT | CONSTELLATION

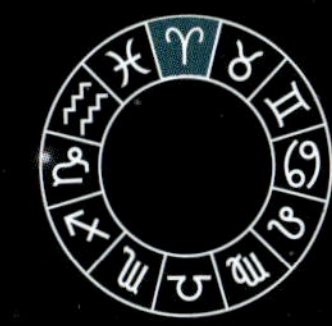

Red
Orange, Magenta

Fire

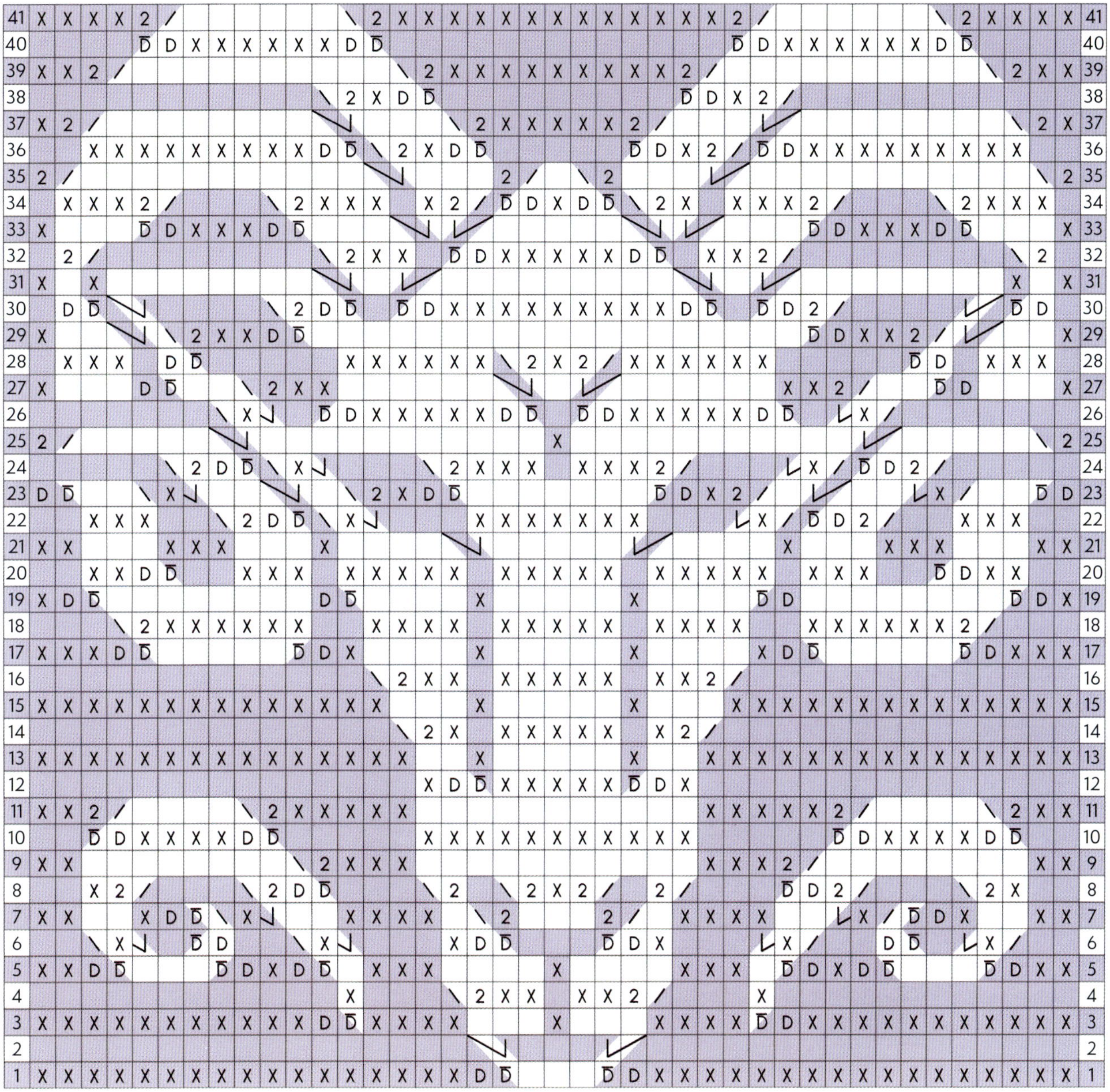

41	X	X	X	X	2	/							|2	X	X	X	X	X	X	X	X	X	X	X	X	X	2	/							|2	X	X	X	X	41
40					D̄	D	X	X	X	X	X	X	D	D̄														D̄	D	X	X	X	X	X	X	D	D̄					40
39	X	X	2	/											|2	X	X	X	X	X	X	X	X	X	2	/											|2	X	X	39
38												|2	X	D	D̄										D̄	D	X	2	/												38
37	X	2	/									|⌋				|2	X	X	X	X	X	2	/				⌊	/									|2	X	37
36			X	X	X	X	X	X	X	X	X	D	D̄	|2	X	D	D̄						D̄	D	X	2	/	D̄	D	X	X	X	X	X	X	X	X	X			36
35	2	/												|⌋				2	/		|2				⌊	/												|2	35
34		X	X	X	2	/				|2	X	X	X		X	2	/	D̄	D	X	D	D̄	|2	X		X	X	X	2	/				|2	X	X	X		34
33	X				D̄	D	X	X	X	D	D̄				|⌋	⌊	/						|⌋	⌊	/				D̄	D	X	X	X	D	D̄				X	33
32		2	/									|2	X	X		D̄	D	X	X	X	X	X	D	D̄		X	X	2	/									|2		32
31	X		X									|⌋		⌊	/										|⌋		⌊	/									X		X	31
30		D	D̄	|⌋					|2	D	D̄		D̄	D	X	X	X	X	X	X	X	X	X	D	D̄		D̄	D	2	/					⌊	/	D̄	D		30
29	X			|⌋	|2	X	X	D	D̄																				D̄	D	X	X	2	/	⌊	/			X	29
28		X	X	X		D	D̄						X	X	X	X	X	X	|2	X	2	/	X	X	X	X	X	X						D̄	D		X	X	X		28
27	X				D	D̄			|2	X	X							|⌋		⌊	/							X	X	2	/			D̄	D				X	27
26								|X	⌋		D̄	D	X	X	X	X	X	D	D̄		D̄	D	X	X	X	X	X	D	D̄		⌊	X	/								26
25	2	/						|⌋												X												⌊	/						|2	25
24						|2	D	D̄	|X	⌋				|2	X	X	X		X	X	X	2	/				⌊	X	/	D̄	D	2	/						24
23	D	D̄			|X	⌋			|⌋		|2	X	D	D̄								D̄	D	X	2	/		⌊	/			⌊	X	/			D̄	D	23
22			X	X	X			|2	D	D̄	|X	⌋				X	X	X	X	X	X	X				⌊	X	/	D̄	D	2	/			X	X	X			22
21	X	X				X	X	X				X					|⌋						⌊	/					X				X	X	X				X	X	21
20			X	X	D	D̄			X	X	X		X	X	X	X	X		X	X	X	X	X		X	X	X	X	X		X	X	X			D̄	D	X	X			20
19	X	D	D̄									D	D̄					X						X					D̄	D									D̄	D	X	19
18				|2	X	X	X	X	X	X			X	X	X	X		X	X	X	X	X		X	X	X	X			X	X	X	X	X	X	2	/				18
17	X	X	X	D	D̄						D̄	D	X					X						X					X	D	D̄						D̄	D	X	X	X	17
16														|2	X	X		X	X	X	X	X		X	X	2	/														16
15	X	X	X	X	X	X	X	X	X	X	X	X	X	X				X						X				X	X	X	X	X	X	X	X	X	X	X	X	X	X	15
14															|2	X		X	X	X	X	X		X	2	/															14
13	X	X	X	X	X	X	X	X	X	X	X	X	X	X	X			X						X			X	X	X	X	X	X	X	X	X	X	X	X	X	X	X	13
12																X	D	D̄	X	X	X	X	X	D̄	D	X																12
11	X	X	2	/					|2	X	X	X	X	X												X	X	X	X	X	2	/					|2	X	X	11
10			D̄	D	X	X	X	X	D	D̄						X	X	X	X	X	X	X	X	X	X	X						D̄	D	X	X	X	X	D	D̄			10
9	X	X									|2	X	X	X												X	X	X	2	/									X	X	9
8			X	2	/				|2	D	D̄				|2		|2	X	2	/		2	/				D̄	D	2	/				|2	X			8
7	X	X			X	D	D̄	|X	⌋			X	X	X	X		|2				2	/		X	X	X	X			⌊	X	/	D̄	D	X			X	X	7
6			|X	⌋		D̄	D			|X	⌋				X	D	D̄				D̄	D	X				⌊	X	/			D	D̄		⌊	X	/			6
5	X	X	D	D̄				D̄	D	X	D	D̄		X	X	X					X					X	X	X		D̄	D	X	D	D̄				D̄	D	X	X	5
4													X				|2	X	X		X	X	2	/				X													4
3	X	X	X	X	X	X	X	X	X	X	X	D	D̄	X	X	X	X				X				X	X	X	X	D̄	D	X	X	X	X	X	X	X	X	X	X	X	3
2																	|⌋					⌊	/																		2
1	X	X	X	X	X	X	X	X	X	X	X	X	X	X	X	X	X	D	D̄				D̄	D	X	X	X	X	X	X	X	X	X	X	X	X	X	X	X	X	X	1

TAURUS

April 20 - May 20

Committed | Patient | Loyal

Taurus is the second sign of the zodiac and is represented by a bull. People born under this earth sign are dependable, trustworthy, and loyal. They have a reputation for being stubborn because they are committed to their beliefs, but they are also very patient and willing to sit through tough times to achieve stability and peace in the long run.

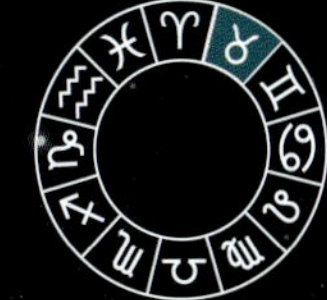

Green
Purple, Brown

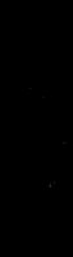

Earth

41	X	X	X	X	X	X	X	X	X	X	X	X	X	X	X	X	X	X	X	X	X	X	X	X	X	X	D	D̄							\	2	X	X	X	X	X	41
40																															\	2	X	X	D	D̄						40
39	X	2	/						D̄	D	X	X	X	X	X	X	X	X	X	X	X	X	X	X	X	X	X	X	X	X	D	D̄					X	X	X	X	X	39
38		D̄	D	X	2	/																											X	X	X	X						38
37	X					X	X	X	X	X	X	X	X	X	X	X	X	X	X	X	X	X	X	X	X	X	X	X	X	X	2	/					X	X	X	X	X	37
36		X	X	X	D	D̄																									D̄	D	X	X	X	X						36
35	X										\	2	X	X	X	X	X	X	X	2	/															D̄	D	X	X	X	X	35
34		\	2	X	X	X	X	X	X	X	D	D̄								D̄	D	X	X	X	X	X	X	X	X	X	X	X	X	2	/							34
33	X	D	D̄										X						X															D̄	D	X	X	X	X	X	X	33
32					\	2	X	X	X	X	2	/	D̄	D	X		X	X		X	X	X	X	X	X	X	X	X	X	2	/											32
31	X	X	X	X	D	D̄					└/				└/				X											└/					\	2	X	X	X	X	X	31
30												X	X	X		X	X	D	D̄	\	2	X	X	2	/					└/				\	X	┘						30
29	X	X	X	2	/					└/				└/						\┘				└/						└	X	/		\┘			\	2	X	X	X	29
28				└	X	/					X	X	X		X	X	2	/	X	D	D̄			D̄	D	X					D̄	D	X	D	D̄	\	X	┘				28
27	X	2	/		└/			2	/	X							└/										\	2	2	/									\	2	X	27
26		└	X	/	D̄	D	X		D	D̄	\	2	X	X	2	/	D̄	D	2	/					D	D̄	\┘			X	X	X	X	X	2	/						26
25	X						D̄	D											└/								\┘								D̄	D	X	X	X	X	X	25
24									\	2	X	X	X	X	X	X	2	/						D̄	D	X	D	D̄														24
23	X	X	X	X	X	X	X	X	D	D̄							D̄	D	X	X	X	2	/							X	X	X	2	/		\	2	X	X	X	X	23
22											X	X	X	X	X	X						D̄	D	X	X	X	X	X	X				D̄	D	X	D	D̄					22
21	X	X	X	X	X	X	X	X	X	X							2	/												X	2	/						\	2	X	X	21
20											X	X	X	X	2	/	D̄	D	X	X	X	X	X	X	2	/	X	X	X			2	/			\	2	X				20
19	X	X	X	X	X	X	X	2	/	X						X									└/					X	X		X	X	X	X			X	X	X	19
18								└/			X	X	X	X	X		X	X	X	X	2	/			D̄	D	X	2	/			X						X	X			18
17	X	X	X	X	X	2	/	D̄	D	X						X					└/								X	X	D	D̄	\	2	2	/			X	X	X	17
16						D̄	D				X	X	X	X	X	D̄	D	X	X	X	D̄	D	X	X	X	X	2	/									X	X	X			16
15	X	X	X	2	/		D̄	D	X	X																	D̄	D	X	X	X	X	X	2	/			D̄	D	X	X	15
14					X	X					X	X	X	X	X	X	X	X	X	X	X	X	X	X	2	/										X	X	X				14
13	X	X	2	/		D̄	D	X	2	/															D̄	D	X	X	X	X	X	X	2	/			D̄	D	X	X	X	13
12			D̄	D	X					X	X	X	X	X	X	2	/			\	2	X	2	/											X	X	X					12
11	X	X			D̄	D	X	X	X							└/				\┘				X	X	X	X	X	X	X	X	2	/			D̄	D	X	\	2	X	11
10		D̄	D	X												└/			X	X		X	X											X	X	X			\┘			10
9	X			D̄	D	X	X	X	D	D̄							X	X			X		D̄	D	X	X	X	X	X	X	2	/			D̄	D	X	X	X		X	9
8		X	X								\	2	X	X	2	/		D̄	D	X											D̄	D	2	/					D̄	D		8
7	X			X	D	D̄	\	2	X	2	/					X				└/		X	X	X	X	X	X	X	2	/			D̄	D	X	X	2	/			X	7
6		X	D	D̄		D̄	D				\	2	X	X	D	D̄	X	2	/	└/									└	X	/						D̄	D	X	X		6
5	X							X	X	X	D	D̄						└/		D̄	D	X	X	X	X	X	2	/		D̄	D	X	X	X	2	/				D̄	D	5
4		\	2	X	X	2	/											└/									└/								D̄	D	X	2	/			4
3	X	D	D̄			D̄	D	X	X	X	X	X	D	D̄				D̄	D	X	X	X	X	X	2	/	D̄	D	X	X	X	X	2	/				D̄	D	X	X	3
2																									└/								D̄	D	X	2	/					2
1	X	X	X	X	X	X	X	X	X	X	X	X	X	X	X	X	X	X	X	X	X	X	X	X	D̄	D	X	2	/							D̄	D	X	X	X	X	1

GEMINI

May 21 – June 20

Adventurous | Expressive | Social

Gemini is the third sign of the zodiac and is represented by twins. People born under this air sign are lively, curious social butterflies who seek adventure and change. Their curious nature allows them to explore a variety of different interests, hobbies, jobs, and relationships, and they're always planning their next big idea. Geminis are big on communication and seek relationships that are intellectually stimulating,

Yellow
Teal, Orange

Air

CANCER

June 21 - July 22

Sensitive | Protective | Intuitive

Cancer is the fourth sign of the zodiac and is represented by a crab. People born under this water sign are deep-feeling emotional beings who are passionate about family, home, and love. They enjoy "nesting" and creating a comfortable and stable home, cooking and preparing meals, and nurturing and protecting everyone in their inner circle.

GLYPH

POWER COLORS

Silver
Pink, Light blue

POSITION

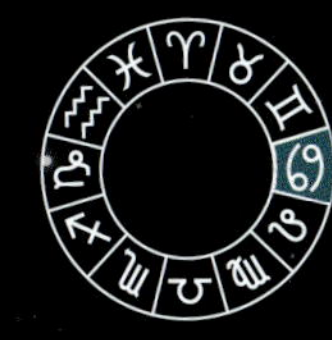

ELEMENT

Water

CONSTELLATION

July 23 – August 22

Courageous | Expressive | Fierce

Leo is the fifth sign of the zodiac and is represented by a lion. People born under this fire sign are noticed when they walk into a room. They thrive in the spotlight, and are confident, expressive beings who often enjoy being performers and entertainers. They are charismatic and warm, and people tend to gravitate to them. Leos are fiercely loyal, and will protect their tribe at all costs.

GLYPH

POWER COLORS

Orange
Golden yellow, Lime

POSITION

ELEMENT

Fire

CONSTELLATION

VIRGO

August 23 - September 22

Hardworking | Analytical | Perfectionist

Virgo is the sixth sign of the zodiac and is represented by a maiden. People born under this earth sign are detail-oriented, hardworking beings who strive for perfection. They want to learn and absorb all the knowledge in the world to better serve their community and personally improve themselves. By nature, Virgos are modest and reserved, and don't like to flaunt their many talents, or stand out in a crowd.

GLYPH

POWER COLORS

Green
Deep blue, Brown

POSITION

ELEMENT

Earth

CONSTELLATION

41	X	X	X	X	X	X	X	X	X	X	X	2	/			\	2	X	X	X	X	X	X	X	X	X	X	X	X	X	X	X	X	X	X	X	X	X	X	X	X	41
40													X		X	X																										40
39	X	X	X	X	2	/		\	2	X	X	X	∟				X	X	X	X	X	X	X	X	X	X	X	X	2	/			\	2	X	X	X	X	X	X	X	39
38								X					D̄	D	2	/																\	X	⌟								38
37	X	X	X	X	X	X	X		2	/	∟				∟											\	2	X	X	X	X	X			X	X	X	X	X	X	X	37
36							∟		D̄	D		X	2	/	D̄	D	X	X	X	X	X	X	X	X	X	D	D̄					D̄	D	X								36
35	X	X	X	X	2	/	∟			∟			∟																					∟	X	/			\	2	X	35
34					D̄	D		2	/	∟	X	/	D̄	D	X	X	2	/							\	2	X	X	X	X	X	2	/			X		X	X			34
33	X	X	2	/			X		X			X					∟								⌟							D̄	D	X	D	D̄	X			X	X	33
32			D̄	D	2	/	D̄	D		X	X		X	X	2	/	D̄	D	2	/																	∟	X	/			32
31	X	X			∟				X			D	D̄		∟				∟																			D̄	D	X	X	31
30		∟	X	/	D̄	D	2	/											D̄	D	X	2	/																			30
29	X			X			∟												⌟			∟																\	2	X	X	29
28		X	X		2	/	D̄	D	X	X	X	X	X	X	X	X	X	D	D̄			D̄	D	X	X	2	/						\	2	X	X	\	X	⌟			28
27	X			X	∟																⌟					∟								⌟				⌟		\	2	27
26		X	D	D̄		X	X	X	X	X	X	X	X	X	X	X	X	X	X	X						∟	X	/				\	X	⌟	\	2	D	D̄	\	2		26
25	D	D̄			X																\	X	⌟				∟						⌟			⌟			X		X	25
24			\	2		2	/					X	X	X	X					\	2						D̄	D	X	X	X	D	D̄	\	2		X	X		X		24
23	X	X	X		X							⌟			∟							X		X	2	/								X		X			X	D̄	D	23
22				X		X	X	X	X	X	X		X	X		X	X	X	X	X	X		X		D̄	D	X	2	/		\	2	X		X		X	X				22
21	X	X	D	D̄	X						D̄	D				⌟						X		X				∟	X	/	D	D̄		X		X			X	X	X	21
20						D	D̄						X	X	X					D̄	D		X							X		D̄	D		X		2	/				20
19	X	X	X	X	X							X										X	∟							⌟			∟		∟		D̄	D	X	X	X	19
18						X	X	X	X	X	X	D̄	D	X	X	X	X	X	X	X	X		D̄	D	X	X	X	X	D	D̄												18
17	X	X	X	X	D	D̄															∟										\	2	X	X	X	X	X	X	X	X	X	17
16							X	X	X	X	D	D̄			D̄	D	X	X	X	X								\	2	X	X											16
15	X	X	X	X	X	D	D̄													∟	X	/				\	2	D	D̄			X	X	X	X	X	X	X	2	/	X	15
14								X	X	2	/					\	2	X	X		∟				\	2				X	X								∟			14
13	X	X	X	X	X	X	D	D̄											D̄	D	D̄	D	X	X	X		X	X	X		D̄	D	X	X	2	/				X	X	13
12									\	2	D	D̄			D̄	D	2	/							∟				∟						D̄	D	X	X	X			12
11	X	X	X	X	X	X	X	X	D	D̄							D̄	D	X	X	X	X	X	X	D̄	D	X	X	D̄	D	X	X	2	/						X	X	11
10											\	2	X	X	2	/																		X	X	X	X	2	/			10
9	X	X	X	X	X	X	X	X	X	X	D	D̄			D̄	D	2	/												\	2	2	/					D̄	D	X	X	9
8																	∟							⌟							⌟	∟										8
7	X			X	X	X	X	X	X	X	X	X	X	X	2	/		\	2	X	X	X	D	D̄	\	2	X	X	X	D	D̄		X	X	X	X	X	X	X	X	X	7
6		\	X	⌟											∟				⌟						X								⌟									6
5	X	D	D̄		\	2	X	X	X	X	X	X	2	/	D̄	D	X	X			\	2	X	X				\	2	X	X	X						\	2	X	X	5
4				\	X	⌟							∟						X	X	D	D̄			X	X	X	D	D̄				X	X	X	X	X	D	D̄			4
3	X	X	X	D	D̄								D̄	D	X	X	X	X					X	X						X	X	D	D̄							X	X	3
2																			\	2	X	X			\	2	X	X	D	D̄									⌟			2
1	X	X	X	X	X	X	X	X	X	X	X	X	X	X	X	X	X	X	D	D̄			X	X	D	D̄					\	2	X	X	X	X	X	X	X	D̄	D	1

LIBRA

September 23 - October 22

Peacekeeper | Empathetic | Fair

Libra is the seventh sign of the zodiac and is represented by scales. People born under this air sign are peacekeepers. They are humanitarians at heart who want to make the world a better place. You'll find a Libra in almost every friend circle and they will often put their own needs aside in order to make sure the people around them are happy. They also need balance and harmony in their home, and beautifying their space is often very important.

GLYPH

POWER COLORS

Pink
Light blue, Lavender

POSITION

ELEMENT

Air

CONSTELLATION

SCORPIO

October 23 – November 21

Passionate | Strong Willed | Confident

Scorpio is the eighth sign of the zodiac and is represented by a scorpion. People born under this water sign are passionate beings who know what they want and are willing to fight for it. Scorpios need to feel in control of their life, and that may come across as domineering, but they are by nature sensitive creatures who crave emotional intimacy. They are also sexually assertive, and take great pride in their appearance.

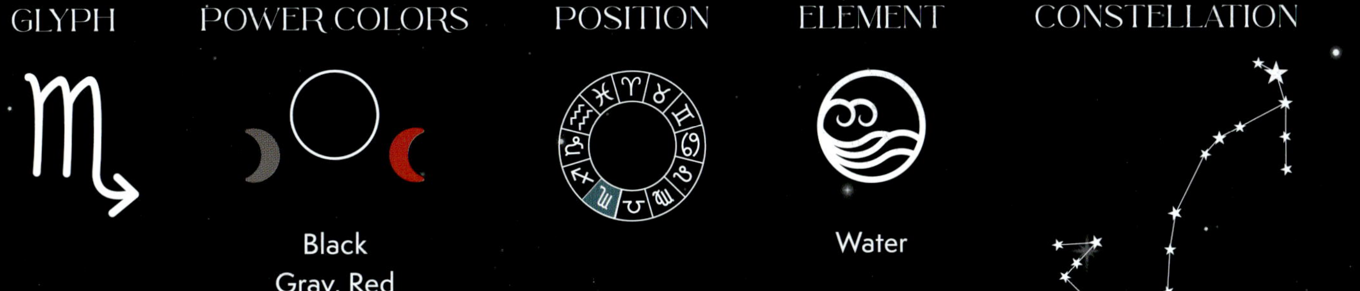
GLYPH
POWER COLORS
POSITION
ELEMENT
CONSTELLATION
Black
Gray, Red
Water

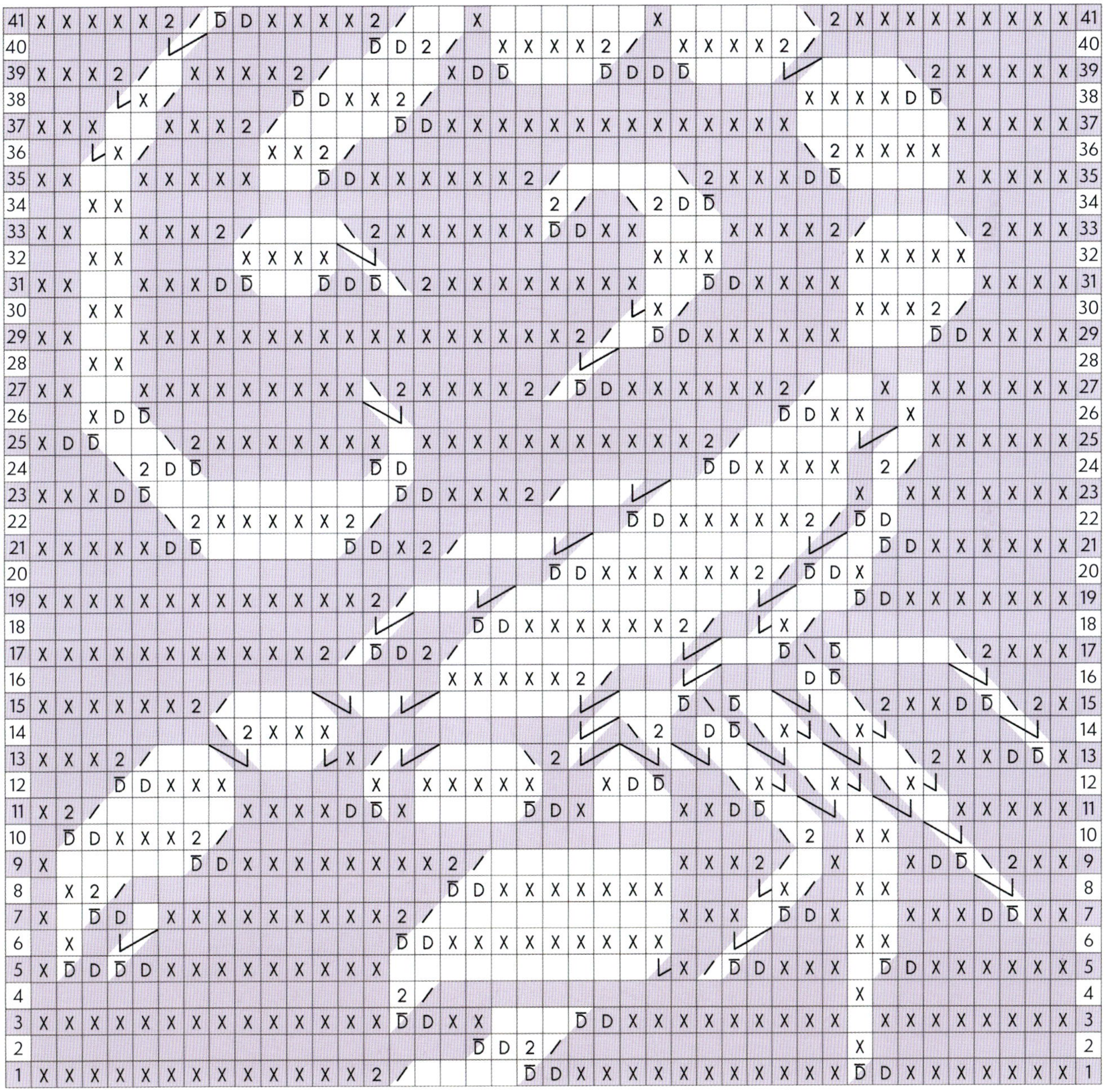

SAGITTARIUS

November 22 - December 21

Dynamic | Explorer | Playful

Sagittarius is the ninth sign of the zodiac and is represented by an archer. People born under this fire sign are dynamic, often with a larger-than-life personality and a big sense of humor. They are always on the move and on a quest for knowledge and discovery. They are big on traveling, exploring the unknown, and experiencing all life has to offer.

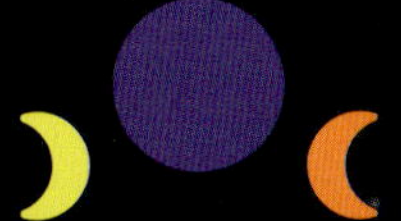

Purple
Yellow, Orange

Fire

CAPRICORN

December 22 – January 19

Ambitious | Driven | Practical

Capricorn is the tenth sign of the zodiac and is represented by a sea goat. People born under this earth sign are ambitious, hard working, and driven to succeed. They have the ability to climb the steepest hills of life's big obstacles, and not let anything stand in their way. They have a lot of goals they want to achieve, and managing their time is very important.

GLYPH

POWER COLORS

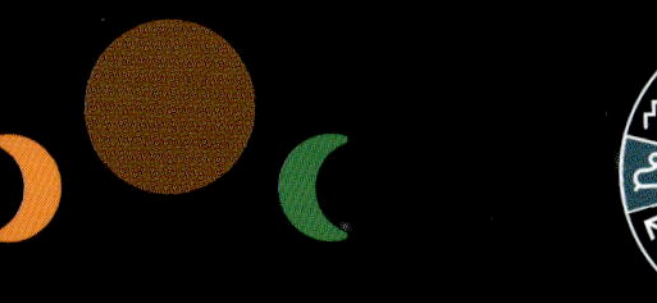

Brown
Orange, Green

POSITION

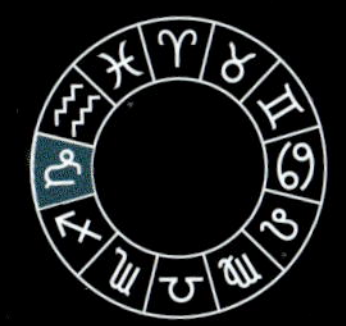

ELEMENT

Earth

CONSTELLATION

41	X	X	X	X	X	X	X	X	X	X	X	X	X	X	X	X	X	X	X	X	X	X	2	/			\	2	X	X	X	X	X	2	/	\	2	X	X	X	X	41
40																							D̄	D	X	X	D	D̄						D̄	D	D	D̄					40
39	X	X	X	X	X	X	X	X	X	X	X	X	X	X	X	X	X	X	X	X	2	/							\	2	X	2	/					\	2	X	X	39
38																					⌊	X	/				\	2	D	D̄		D̄	D	2	/		\	2				38
37	X	X	X	X	X	X	X	X	X	X	X	2	/	X	X	X	X	X	2	/		D̄	D	X	X	X	X				X				X	X	X		X	X	X	37
36												⌊/							⌊	X	/							2	/				\	2			⌊/					36
35	X	X	X	X	X	X	X	X	X	2	/	⌊/		X	2	/				D̄	D	X	X	X	X	X	X	⌊/					\⌋		X	X	D̄	D	X	X	X	35
34										⌊/		⌊/																D̄	D	X	X	X	D	D̄								34
33	X	X	X	X	X	X	X	2	/	⌊/		⌊/		X	X	X	X	X	X	X	X	D	D̄			\	2								2	/			D̄	D	X	33
32								⌊/		⌊/		⌊/												\	2	X				X	X	X				X	2	/				32
31	X	X	X	X	X	X	X		X		X		X	X	X	X	X	X	X	X	X	X	X	D	D̄		X	\	X	⌋		⌊	X	/	X		D̄	D	X	X	X	31
30								X		X		X																D	D̄		X		D̄	D								30
29	X	X	X	X	X	X	X		X		X		X	X	X	X	X	X	X	X	X	X	X	X	X	X	X			X		X			X	X	X	X	X	X	X	29
28								X		X		X																\	X	⌋	X	⌊	X	/								28
27	X	X	X	X	X	X	X		X		X	⌊/				⌊/		⌊/		D̄	D	X	X	X	X	X	\	2						X	X	X	X	X	X	X	X	27
26																⌊/		⌊/									D	D̄	\⌋			⌊/										26
25	X	X	X	X	X	2	/			⌊/						⌊/		D̄	D	X	X	X	2	/					\⌋		X	⌊/			X	X	X	X	X	X	X	25
24						D̄	D	2	/							⌊/							D̄	D	X	X	X	X	D	D̄		D̄	D	X								24
23	X	X	X	2	/			⌊/								D̄	D	X	X	2	/														X	X	X	X	X	X	X	23
22				D̄	D	2	/													D̄	D	X	X	X	X	X	X	X	X	X	X	X	X	X								22
21	X	2	/				X	X	X	X	X	X	X	X	X	X	X	2	/																X	2	/			\	2	21
20			X	X	2	/												D̄	D	X	X	X	X	X	X	X	X	X	X	X	X	X	X	X		D̄	D	X	X	X		20
19	2	/				X	X	2	/						\	3	/																								X	19
18		X	X	2	/			D̄	D	X	X	X	X	X	D	D̄	\	2	X	X	X	X	X		X	X	X	X	2	/	X	X	X	X	X	2	/	X	X	X		18
17	X				X	2	/										X							X					⌊/								X				X	17
16		X	X	X		D̄	D	X	2	/			X	X	X	X		X	X	X	X	X	X		X	X	2	/	D̄	D	X	X	X	X	2	/		X	2	/		16
15	X				X				D̄	D	X	X					X							X				\⌋							D̄	D	X			X	X	15
14		X	X	X		X	X	X				D̄	D	X	X	X		X	X	X	X	X	X		X	X	X	D	D̄									X	X			14
13	X				\⌋				\	3	/						X							X											X	X	X			X	X	13
12		X	X	X	D	D̄				D̄	D	X	X	X	2	/	D̄	D	X	X	X	X	X		X	X	X	X	X	X	X	X	X	D	D̄							12
11	D	D̄													⌊/									D	D̄											2	/			X	X	11
10			\	2	X	X	X	X	X	X	X	2	/		D̄	D	X	X	X	X	X	X	D	D̄								D̄	D	X	X		X	X	X			10
9	X	X	D	D̄								⌊/															D̄	D	X	X	X				D̄	D	D̄			X	X	9
8												D̄	D	X	X	X	X	X	X	X	X	X	X	X	2	/					D̄	D	2	/				\	2			8
7	X	X	X	X	X	X	D	D̄																	D̄	D	X	X	2	/			D̄	D	X	X	X	D	D̄	X	X	7
6									\	2	X	X	X	X	X	X	X	X	X	2	/									X	2	/										6
5	X	X	X	X	X	X	X	X	D	D̄										D̄	D	X	X	X	X	X			\⌋		D̄	D	X	X	X	X	X	X	X	X	X	5
4																											X	X	X													4
3	X	X	X	X	X	X	X	X	X	X	X	X	X	X	X	X	X	X	X	X	X	X	X	X	X	X			D̄	D	X	X	X	X	X	X	X	X	X	X	X	3
2																											2	/														2
1	X	X	X	X	X	X	X	X	X	X	X	X	X	X	X	X	X	X	X	X	X	X	X	X	X	X	D̄	D	X	X	X	X	X	X	X	X	X	X	X	X	X	1

AQUARIUS

January 20 - February 18

Eccentric | Imaginative | Humanitarian

Aquarius is the eleventh sign of the zodiac and is represented by a water-bearer. People born under this air sign are free-spirited, and have a unique outlook on life. They often have abstract ideas, creative solutions, and offer a unique perspective to solving problems. They are rebels who march to the beat of their own drum, and are passionate about human rights.

Blue
Lavender, Teal

Air

PISCES

February 19 - March 20

Emotional | Imaginative | Compassionate

Pisces is the twelfth sign of the zodiac and is represented by fish. People born under this water sign are deeply empathetic and sensitive to other people's feelings. They are emotional beings with one foot in reality and one foot in a fantasy world, or two fish swimming in opposite directions. They are artistic dreamers with wild imaginations, and are often very creative.

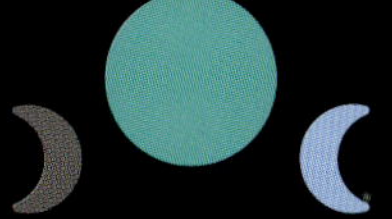

Aquamarine
Gray, Light blue

Water

41	X	X	X	X	X	X	X	X	X	X	X	X	X	X	X	X	2	/				\	2	X	X	X	X	X	X	X	X	X	X	X	X	X	X	X	X	X	X	41
40																	D̄	D	X	X	X	D	D̄																			40
39	X	2	/	X	X	X	X	X	2	/			X	X	2	/										\	2	X	X	X	X	X	X	X	X	X	X	X	X	X	X	39
38		└/							└/						└	X	/		\	2	X	2	/																			38
37	X		X	X	X	X	2	/	D̄	D	X	2	/			D̄	D	X	X			└/							X							\	\	3	X	X	X	37
36			\┘				└/															D̄	D	X	X	X	X	D	D̄	\	2	D	D̄			X	D	D̄				36
35	X	D	D̄				D̄	D	X	X	X	X	X	X	X	2	/														\┘								\	2	X	35
34																D̄	D	X	X	X	X	X	X	X	X	X	X	X	X	D	D̄	\	2	X	X	X	X	X	D	D̄		34
33	X	X	X	X	X	X	X	X	2	/																							\┘							D̄	D	33
32									D̄	D	X	X	X	X	X	X	X	2	/									D̄	D	X	X	X		X	X	2	/	2	/			32
31	X	X	X	X	X	2	/	X										└/								└/							X			└/		D̄	D	X	X	31
30						D̄	D		X	2	/				\	2	X		X	X	X	X	X	X	X		X	X	X	X	2	/	D̄	D	X	└/						30
29	X	X	X	2	/			X		└/		\	2	X	D	D̄	└/								└/							X				D̄	D	X	X	X	X	29
28				D̄	D	X	X		X		X	X					D̄	D	X	2	/				D̄	D	X	X	X	X	X		X	2	/							28
27	X	X	X					X	└/				X	X	X	X				└/												X		D̄	D	X	X	X	X	X	X	27
26				X	X	X	X		D̄	D	X	X				└	X	/																								26
25	X	2	/				D̄	D					2	/			D̄	D	X	X	2	/							D̄	D	X	X	X	X	X	X	X	X	X	X	X	25
24			X	X	2	/			X	X	X	X									D̄	D	X	X	X	X	2	/														24
23	2	/			D̄	D	X	D	D̄				X	X	X	X	2	/									D̄	D	X	2	/	X	X	X	X	X	X	X	X	X	X	23
22		2	/							X	X	X						2	/												X											22
21	X	D̄	D	X	X	X	X	X	D	D̄		D̄	D	X	X	X	X	D̄	D	X	X	X	2	/	X	X	X	X	2	/		\	2	X	X	X	X	X	2	/	X	21
20											X												D̄	D						X	X	X							D̄	D		20
19	X	X	X	X	X	X	X	X	X	X	D̄	D	X	2	/									D̄	D	X	X	X	X				\	2	X	2	/			D̄	D	19
18														D̄	D	X	X	X	X	2	/									X	X	X	X			D̄	D	X	X			18
17	X	X	X	X	X	X	X	X	X	X	X	2	/							D̄	D	X	X	2	/			D̄	D					2	/				D̄	D	X	17
16																								└	X	/				X	X	2	/		X	X	X	X				16
15	X	X	X	X	X	X	2	/		X											└/					X	X	X	X			└/		X					X	X	X	15
14							D̄	D	X		X	X	X	X	X	2	/				D̄	D	X	2	/					X	X		X		X	X	2	/				14
13	X	X	X	X	2	/				X						└/								└/		\	2	X	D	D̄	└/			X			D̄	D	X	X	X	13
12					└/		X	2	/	D̄	D	X	X	X	X		X	X	X	X	X	X	X		X	D	D̄				D̄	D	X		2	/						12
11	X	X	2	/	└/				X						└/								└/											X	D̄	D	X	X	X	X	X	11
10			D̄	D	D̄	D	X	X		X	X	X	2	/									D̄	D	X	X	X	X	X	X	X	2	/									10
9	2	/								\┘																						D̄	D	X	X	X	X	X	X	X	X	9
8		\	2	X	X	X	X	X	D	D̄	\	2	X	X	X	X	X	X	X	X	X	X	X	X	2	/																8
7	X	D	D̄									\┘													D̄	D	X	X	X	X	X	X	X	2	/				\	2	X	7
6				\	\	3			\	2	D	D̄	\	2	X	X	X	X	2	/														└/						\┘		6
5	X	X	X	X	D	D̄							X						└/				X	X	2	/			D̄	D	X	2	/	D̄	D	X	X	X	X		X	5
4																			D̄	D	X	D	D̄		└	X	/					└/							└/			4
3	X	X	X	X	X	X	X	X	X	X	X	X	X	X	D	D̄										D̄	D	X	X			D̄	D	X	X	X	X	X	D̄	D	X	3
2																			\	2	X	X	X	2	/																	2
1	X	X	X	X	X	X	X	X	X	X	X	X	X	X	X	X	X	X	D	D̄				D̄	D	X	X	X	X	X	X	X	X	X	X	X	X	X	X	X	X	1

GLYPH CHARTS

Aries

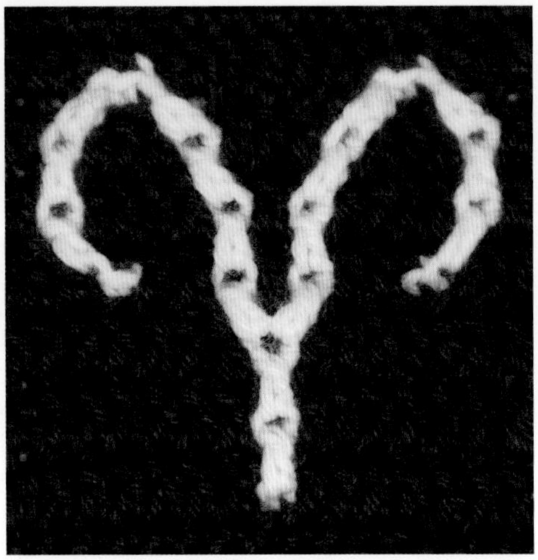

13	X	2	/		\	2	X	X	X	2	/		\	2	X	13
12																12
11	X		X	X	X		X	X	X		X	X	X		X	11
10		X												X		10
9	X		X	X	X	X		X		X	X	X	X		X	9
8							X		X							8
7	X	D	D̄		X	X		X		X	X		D̄	D	X	7
6							\	∇	/							6
5	X	X	X	X	X	X	X		X	X	X	X	X	X	X	5
4								X								4
3	X	X	X	X	X	X	X		X	X	X	X	X	X	X	3
2								X								2
1	X	X	X	X	X	X	X		X	X	X	X	X	X	X	1

Taurus

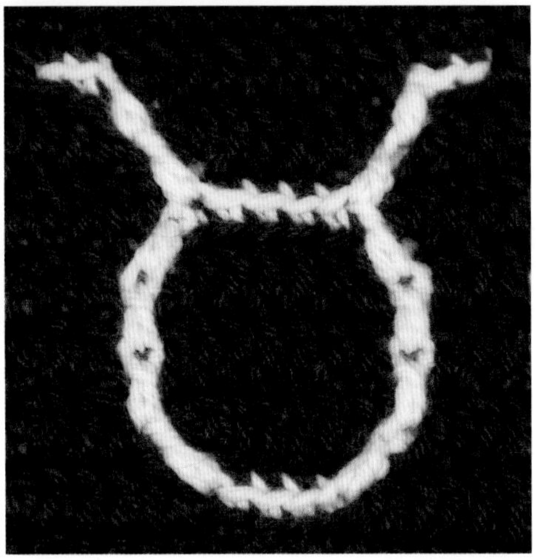

13	X			\	2	X	X	X	X	X	2	/			X	13
12				X								X				12
11	X	X	D	D̄	\	2	X	X	X	2	/	D̄	D	X	X	11
10																10
9	X	X	X	2	/						\	2	X	X	X	9
8																8
7	X	X	X		X	X	X	X	X	X	X		X	X	X	7
6				X								X				6
5	X	X	X		X	X	X	X	X	X	X		X	X	X	5
4				X								X				4
3	X	X	D	D̄	\	2	X	X	X	2	/	D̄	D	X	X	3
2																2
1	X	X	X	X	D	D̄				D̄	D	X	X	X	X	1

Gemini

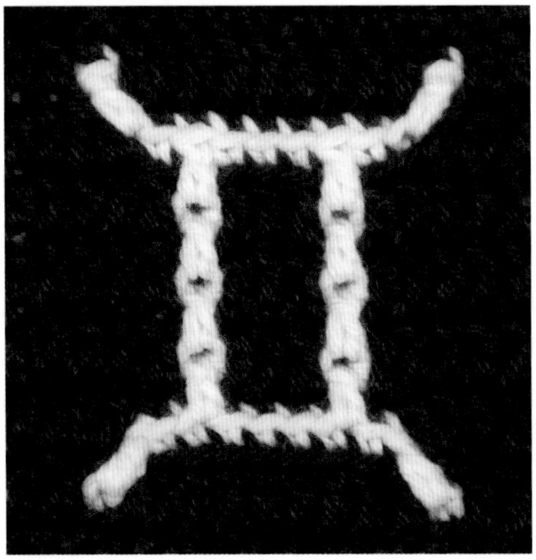

13	X	X		X	X	X	X	X	X	X	X	X		X	X	13
12																12
11	X	X	D	D̄								D̄	D	X	X	11
10						X				X						10
9	X	X	X	X	X		X	X	X		X	X	X	X	X	9
8						X				X						8
7	X	X	X	X	X		X	X	X		X	X	X	X	X	7
6						X				X						6
5	X	X	X	X	X		X	X	X		X	X	X	X	X	5
4						X				X						4
3	X	X	2	/								\	2	X	X	3
2																2
1	X	X		X	X	X	X	X	X	X	X	X		X	X	1

Cancer

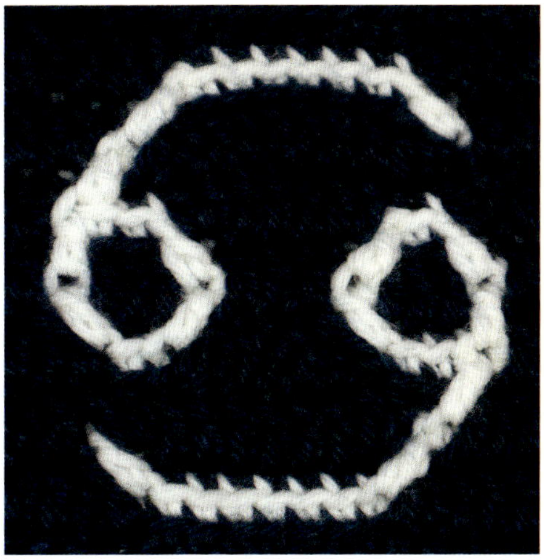

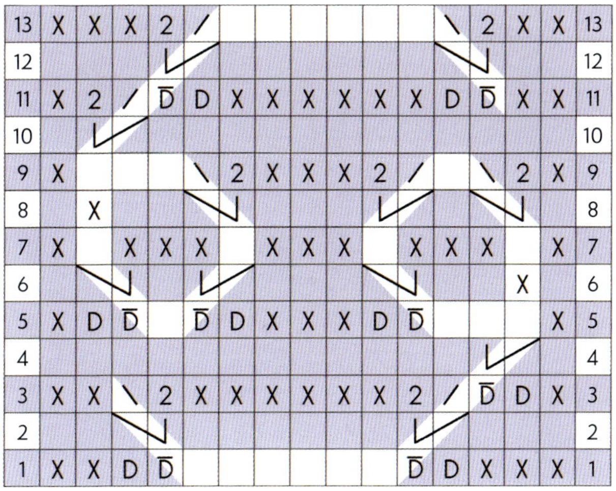

13	X	X	X	2	/							\	2	X	X	13
12																12
11	X	2	/	D̄	D	X	X	X	X	X	X	D	D̄	X	X	11
10																10
9	X				\	2	X	X	X	2	/		\	2	X	9
8		X														8
7	X		X	X	X		X	X	X		X	X	X		X	7
6														X		6
5	X	D	D̄		D̄	D	X	X	X	D	D̄				X	5
4																4
3	X	X	\	2	X	X	X	X	X	X	2	/	D̄	D	X	3
2																2
1	X	X	D	D̄							D̄	D	X	X	X	1

Leo

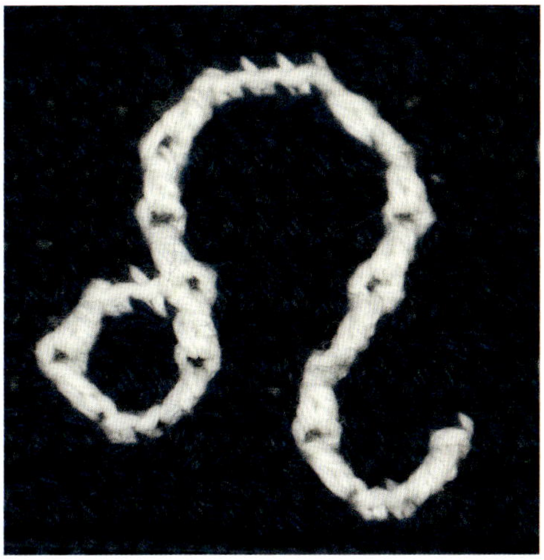

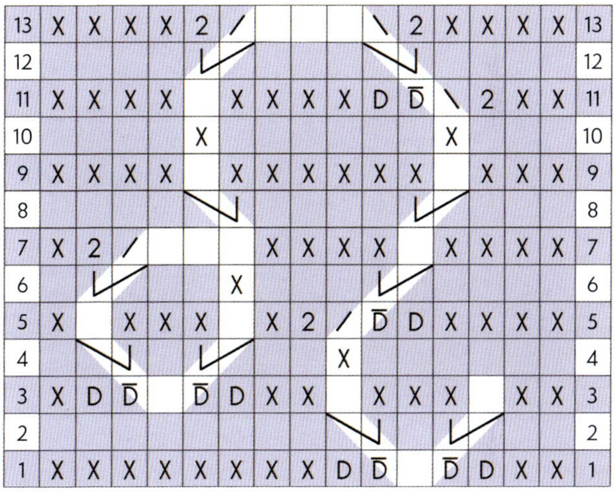

13	X	X	X	X	2	/			\	2	X	X	X	X		13
12																12
11	X	X	X	X		X	X	X	X	D	D̄	\	2	X	X	11
10					X							X				10
9	X	X	X	X		X	X	X	X	X	X		X	X	X	9
8																8
7	X	2	/				X	X	X	X		X	X	X	X	7
6						X										6
5	X		X	X	X		X	2	/	D̄	D	X	X	X	X	5
4									X							4
3	X	D	D̄		D̄	D	X	X		X	X	X		X	X	3
2																2
1	X	X	X	X	X	X	X	X	D	D̄		D̄	D	X	X	1

Virgo

13	X			\	2		\	2		\	2	X	X	X	X	13
12				X			X			X						12
11	X	X	X		D̄	D		D̄	D		X	\	2	X	X	11
10				X			X			X	D̄	\	D̄			10
9	X	X	X		X	X		X	X		D̄	D		X	X	9
8				X			X			X			X			8
7	X	X	X		X	X		X	X		X	X		X	X	7
6				X			X			X			X			6
5	X	X	X		X	X		X	X		2	/	D̄	D	X	5
4										X						4
3	X	X	X	X	X	X	X	X	X			X	X	X	X	3
2																2
1	X	X	X	X	X	X	X		D̄	D	D	D̄			X	1

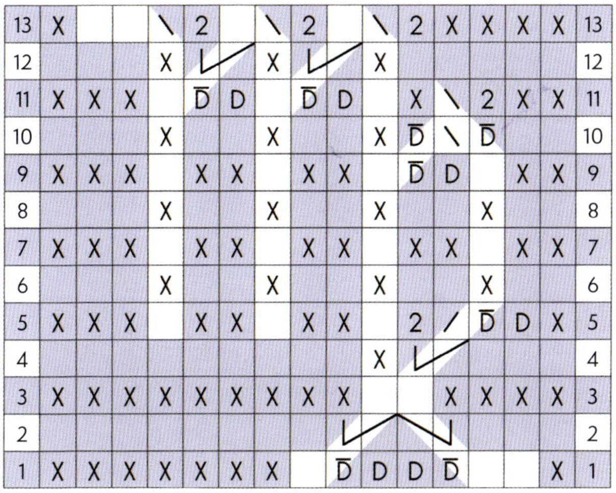

Libra

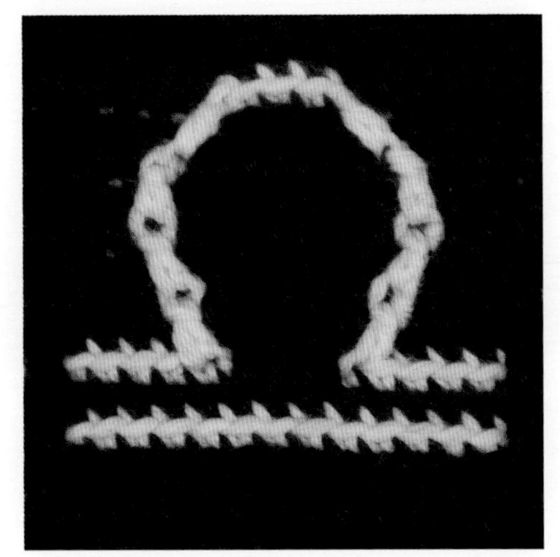

13	X	X	X	X	2	/				\	2	X	X	X	X	13
12																12
11	X	X	2	/	D̄	D	X	X	X	D	D̄	\	2	X	X	11
10				X								X				10
9	X	X	X		X	X	X	X	X	X	X		X	X	X	9
8																8
7	X	X	X	X		X	X	X	X	X		X	X	X	X	7
6																6
5	X						X	X	X						X	5
4																4
3	X														X	3
2																2
1	X	X	X	X	X	X	X	X	X	X	X	X	X	X	X	1

Scorpio

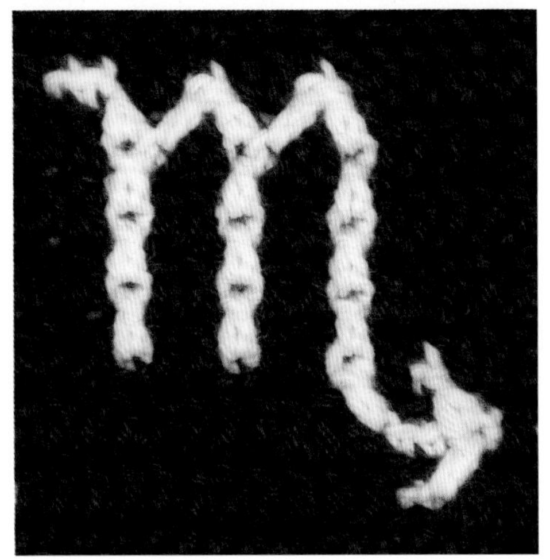

13	X			\	2		\	2		\	2	X	X	X	X	13
12				X			X			X						12
11	X	X	X		D̄	D		D̄	D		X	X	X	X	X	11
10				X			X			X						10
9	X	X	X		X	X		X	X		X	X	X	X	X	9
8				X			X			X						8
7	X	X	X		X	X		X	X		X	X	X	X	X	7
6				X			X			X						6
5	X	X	X		X	X		X	X		X		\	2	X	5
4																4
3	X	X	X	X	X	X	X	X	X	D	D̄				X	3
2																2
1	X	X	X	X	X	X	X	X	X	X	X		D̄	D	X	1

Sagittarius

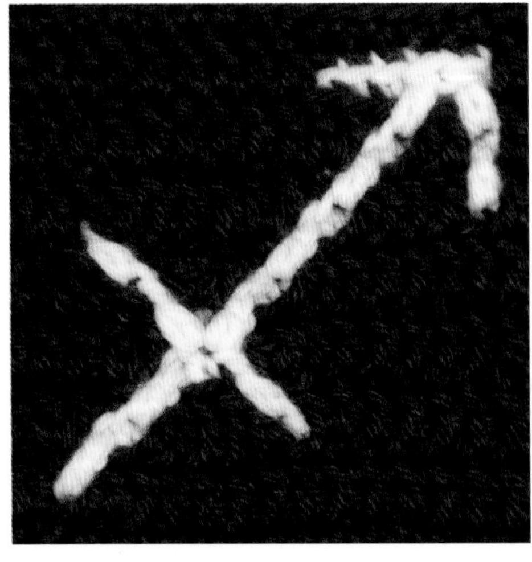

13	X	X	X	X	X	X	X	X	X						X	13
12														X		12
11	X	X	X	X	X	X	X	X	X	2	/	D̄	D		X	11
10														X		10
9	X	X	\	2	X	X	X	2	/	D̄	D	X	X		X	9
8																8
7	X	X	D	D̄	\	▽	/	D̄	D	X	X	X	X	X	X	7
6					\	▽	/									6
5	X	X	X	2	/		\	2	X	X	X	X	X	X	X	5
4																4
3	X	2	/	D̄	D	X	D	D̄	\	2	X	X	X	X	X	3
2																2
1	X	D̄	D	X	X	X	X	X	X	X	X	X	X	X	X	1

Capricorn

13	X			X	2	/		\	2	X	X	X	X	X	X	13
12			X					X								12
11	X	X		X		X	X		X	X	X	X	X	X	X	11
10			\	▽	/			X								10
9	X	X	X		X	X	X		X	X	X	X	X	X	X	9
8				X												8
7	X	X	X		X	X	X	X		2	/		\	2	X	7
6				X					\	▽	/					6
5	X	X	X		X	X	X	X	X		\	2	X		X	5
4										X						4
3	X	X	X	X	X	X	X	X	X		D	D̄	D̄	D	X	3
2																2
1	X	X	X	X	X				D̄	D	X	X	X	X	X	1

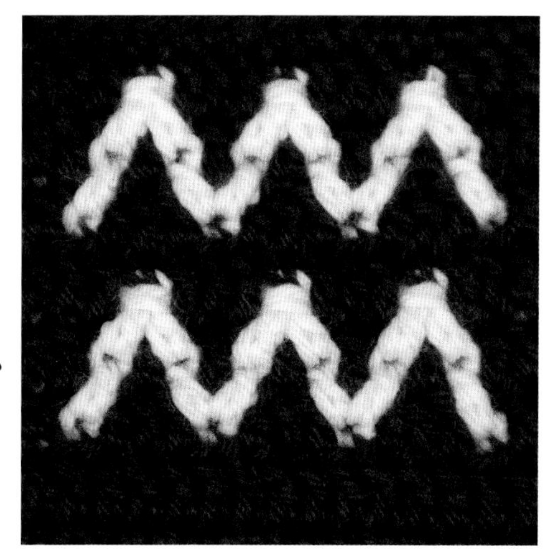

13	X	X	X		X	X	X		X	X	X		X	X	X	13
12			D̄	\	D̄		D̄	\	D̄		D̄	\	D̄			12
11	X	X		X		X		X		X		X		X	X	11
10					\	▽	/		\	▽	/					10
9	X		X	X	X		X	X	X		X	X	X		X	9
8																8
7	X	X	X		X	X	X		X	X	X		X	X	X	7
6			D̄	\	D̄		D̄	\	D̄		D̄	\	D̄			6
5	X	X		X		X		X		X		X		X	X	5
4					\	▽	/		\	▽	/					4
3	X		X	X	X		X	X	X		X	X	X		X	3
2																2
1	X	X	X	X	X	X	X	X	X	X	X	X	X	X	X	1

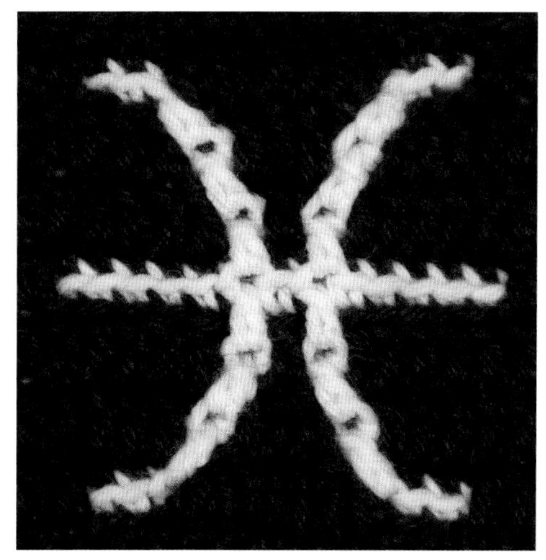

13	X	X			\	2	X	X	X	2	/			X	X	13
12																12
11	X	X	X	X	X		X	X	X		X	X	X	X	X	11
10																10
9	X	X	X	X	X	X		X		X	X	X	X	X	X	9
8							X		X							8
7	X														X	7
6							X		X							6
5	X	X	X	X	X	X		X		X	X	X	X	X	X	5
4																4
3	X	X	X	X	X		X	X	X		X	X	X	X	X	3
2																2
1	X	X			D̄	D	X	X	X	D	D̄			X	X	1

GLYPH

Projects

WHAT'S YOUR SIGN DRINK SLEEVES

Express your celestial individuality and mark your beverages with these colorblock drink sleeves. Bring one to your favorite coffee shop to save on cardboard sleeves, and keep your drink hot and your hands cool. These colorful sleeves are great for beginners; they are crocheted in the round with a slight increase to fit snugly onto a standard paper coffee cup!

YARN USED:

Berroco Modern Cotton™, cotton/modal rayon blend, worsted 4 weight/aran

- Color A: 1 skein (about 36yd/33m or 12yd/11m per color) in three different colors
- Color B: 1 skein (about 30yd/28m) Longspur (black)

HOOK USED:

US H/8 (5mm)

TOOLS & MATERIALS:

Stitch markers

Tapestry needle

GAUGE:

18 stitches and 18 rows = 4in (10cm)

DIMENSIONS:

Approx. 3½in (9cm) tall

9½in (24cm) circumference

FOUNDATION CHAIN

Begin your Foundation Chain in color A (background color) with 38 chains.

FOUNDATION ROW

Your first round is color A (background), and second round color B (glyph color), as indicated in the numbered column of the charts. Each round in this pattern will alternate colors.

Round 1: Chain 1, and SC into the second chain from the hook. SC to the end (39 SCs total).

Follow the instructions in **Working in the Round From Foundation Row** to join Round 1, switch colors, and add Round 2 (all SCs). All remaining rounds will follow the Working in the Round instructions for joining and switching colors.

FOLLOWING THE CHARTS

Choose any Glyph Chart from the Glyph Charts section and then follow the instructions using the rows from the chart you have chosen.

Round 3: 12 DCs, Chart Row 1, 12 DCs. There will be 39 stitches in total.

Round 4: 12 SCs, Chart Row 2, 12 SCs.

Round 5: 2 DCs same stitch, 11 DCs, Chart Row 3, 11 DCs, 2 DCs same stitch. There will now be 41 stitches in total.

Round 6: 13 SCs, Chart Row 4, 13 SCs.

Round 7: Switch to next color A. 13 DCs, Chart Row 5, 13 DCs.

Round 8: 13 SCs, Chart Row 6, 13 SCs.

Round 9: 13 DCs, Chart Row 7, 13 DCs.

Round 10: 13 SCs, Chart Row 8, 13 SCs.

Round 11: 2 DCs same stitch, 12 DCs, Chart Row 9, 12 DCs, 2 DCs same stitch. There will now be 43 stitches in total.

Round 12: 14 SCs, Chart Row 10, 14 SCs.

Round 13: Switch to next color A. 14 DCs, Chart Row 11, 14 DCs.

Round 14: 14 SCs, Chart Row 12, 14 SCs.

Round 15: 14 DCs, Chart Row 13, 14 DCs.

Round 16: Do not switch colors. All SCs, back loops only.

Fasten off, tie inside tails together and weave in.

Placing markers to position the glyph chart

Back of drink sleeve

STARLIGHT POUCHES

Design your own night sky with this starry, crossbody drawstring pouch. This pouch is crocheted in the round and features a glyph of your choice on both sides, with lots of little stars crocheted randomly to your liking! It's the perfect size for a night out to carry your cell phone and other little necessities, and the tasseled drawstring side-closure keeps your items secure.

YARN USED:

Berroco Pima 100™, 100% cotton, worsted 4 weight/aran)

- Color A: 1 skein (about 400yd/366m) Black Eyed Susan (black) or Blue Flax (purple)
- Color B: 1 skein (about 65yd/60m) Yarrow (white)

HOOK USED:

US H/8 (5mm)

TOOLS & MATERIALS:

Stitch markers

Tapestry needle

GAUGE:

19 stitches and 19 rows = 4in (10cm)

DIMENSIONS:

About 7½ x 5in (19 x 12.5cm)

FOUNDATION CHAIN

Begin your Foundation Chain in color A (background color) with 50 chains.

FOUNDATION ROW

Your first round is color A (background), and second round color B (glyph color), as indicated in the numbered column of the charts.

Round 1: Chain 1, and SC into the second chain from the hook. SC to the end (50 SCs total).

Follow the instructions in **Working in the Round From Foundation Row** to join Round 1, switch colors, and add Round 2 (all SCs). All remaining rounds will follow the Working in the Round instructions for joining and switching colors.

RANDOM STARS

This begins the mosaic section, and all DCs will be overlay stitches.

Round 3: Add 1 DC in each stitch to the end, and randomly add SC stitches to create "stars". Be sure to space out the SCs with the majority of stitches being DCs.

Round 4: Add 1 SC in each stitch to the end.

Rounds 5 to 12: Repeat Rounds 3 and 4, four more times.

FOLLOWING THE CHART

The middle section of the pouch continues the random star pattern (Rounds 3 and 4 repeated) with a Glyph Chart centered on both sides. I recommend using stitch markers as a visual guide so you can easily see where the chart starts and ends. Skip the first 5 stitches, mark 15 stitches for the front chart, skip 10 stitches, mark 15 stitches for the back chart, skip the last 5 stitches.

Continue the random star pattern for the first 5 stitches in the round. Begin following any of the Glyph Charts from Row 1, all 15 stitches across. Continue the random star pattern for the next 10 stitches. Add Row 1 of the Glyph Chart again, and finish with 5 random star stitches. Follow the Glyph Chart from Rows 1–13.

Continue adding random star rounds starting with Round 4 then Round 3, and repeat four times in total.

Fasten off, tie inside tails together and weave in.

EYELETS

Do not switch colors after the last join. Cut the color B strand leaving about a 6in (15cm) tail end. Continue to use color A for the remainder of the pouch. Work all remaining stitches in BOTH LOOPS.

Eyelet Round: Chain 2, 2 DCs, chain 2, skip 2, [4 DCs, chain 2, skip 2] 7 times, 3 DCs, join.

Last Round: SC around, working 2 SCs in each eyelet, join.

Fasten off.

Glyph chart marked with stitch markers on pouch base

Adding eyelets to the top of the pouch

FINISHING

To close the bottom of the pouch, turn the pouch inside out and starting from the seam connect both sides together with slip stitches.

STRAP

Leave approx. 12in (30cm) starting tail for attaching to the base of the bag.

Chain 7.

Row 1: Starting in second chain from hook, 6 SCs. Chain 1, turn.

Row 2: 6 SCs, chain 1, turn.

Repeat Row 2 another 200 times or to desired length. Keep in mind the strap will stretch.

Attach the strap using a tapestry needle and double whip stitch it to the base, centered across 6 stitches along the seam and opposite side (**A**).

A

DRAWSTRING

Leave a 4in (10cm) tail and holding 2 strands together, chain 65. Leave a 4in (10cm) tail at end and fasten off. Cut 8in (20cm) strands of both colors to create extra tassels, two of each color. Folded in half, attach to the last stitch of the chain (**B**) and flip the tails in together to make a tassel (**C**). Repeat for other end.

From the seam side, weave half of the chain through the front holes of the pouch and the other half through the back holes of the pouch. Tie a loose knot on the side to close.

B

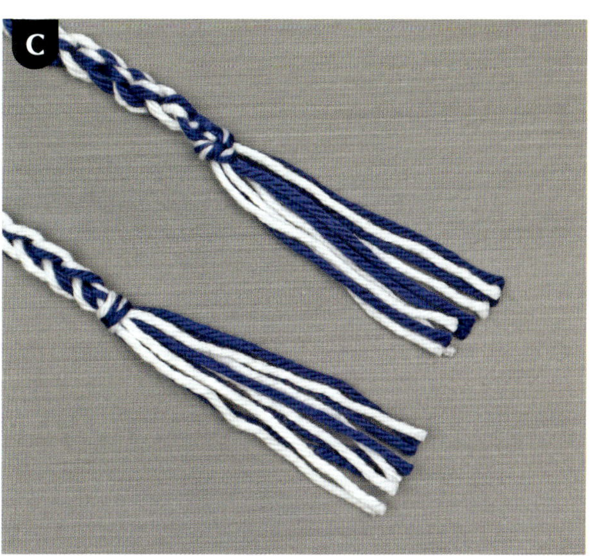
C

GLYPH BEANIES

Stay warm while star-gazing in this cozy glyph beanie. This bold yet simple design features a wide mosaic crochet brim crocheted in the round, with classic ribbed stitching crocheted vertically and gathered at the top.

Choose your sign

You can use any of the glyphs for this beanie – decide which star sign you want to feature and use the relevant chart from the Glyph Charts section.

YARN USED:

Berroco Vintage® Chunky, wool/acrylic blend, Bulky 5 weight/chunky

- Color A: 2 skeins (about 155yd/142m) Cast Iron (black)
- Color B: 1 skein (about 40yd/37m) Dove (gray) or Jade (teal)

HOOK USED:

US K/10½ (6.5mm)

TOOLS & MATERIALS:

Stitch markers

Tapestry needle

Pom-pom maker (optional)

GAUGE:

15 stitches and 15 rows = 4in (10cm)

DIMENSIONS:

About 9in (23cm) tall, 4in (10cm) brim, 20in (51cm) circumference

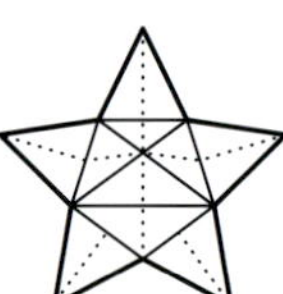

FOUNDATION CHAIN

The brim of the beanie follows a full Glyph Chart repeated 5 times around. 15 x 5 = 75.

Begin your Foundation Chain in color A (background color) with 75 chains.

For a smaller size, begin your Foundation Chain in color A (background color) with 70 chains and skip the last stitch of every row in the chart (you can use a sticky note to cover the last stitch column to help keep track of your stitches). The glyphs will be 14 stitches wide.

FOUNDATION ROW

Your first round is color A (background), and second round color B (glyph color), as indicated in the numbered column of the charts.

Round 1: Chain 1, and SC into the second chain from the hook. SC to the end (75 SCs total).

Follow the instructions in **Working in the Round From Foundation Row** to join Round 1, switch colors, and add Round 2 (all SCs). All remaining rounds will follow the Working in the Round instructions for joining and switching colors.

FOLLOWING THE CHART

Begin following any of the Glyph Charts from Row 1, all 15 stitches across. When crocheting the smaller size beanie, ignore the last stitch of every row. Repeat the row 5 times in total. Follow the chart from Rows 1–13.

Do not switch colors after Row 13. Cut the color B strand leaving about a 6in (15cm) tail end. Continue to use color A for the remainder of the beanie.

Chain 21. All remaining SCs will be back loop only.

Row 1: Starting in the second chain from hook add 20 SCs. 2 slip stitches in next 2 stitches of beanie brim. Turn.

Row 2: Skip 2 slip stitches. Add 20 SCs to the SC section. Chain 1, turn.

Row 3: Add 20 SCs. 2 slip stitches in next 2 stitches of beanie brim. Turn.

Repeat Rows 2 and 3 around beanie brim (**A**).

For the last row of ribbing, after last 2 slip stitches, join first and last rows together by adding 20 SCs into the BLO.

Leave a 24–36in (60–90cm) tail, cut and fasten off.

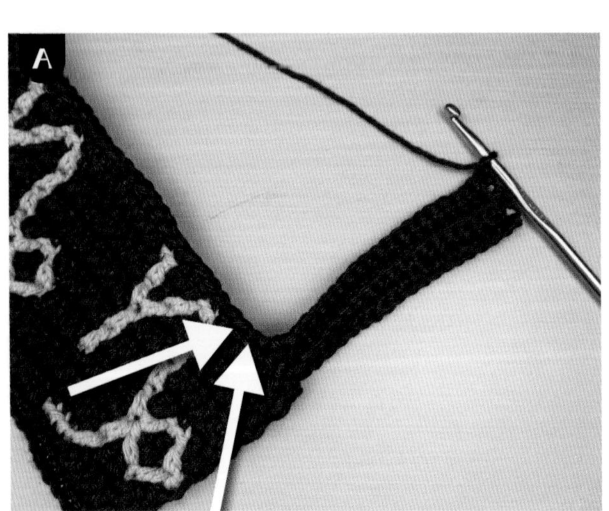

Ribbing section showing 4 rows of SCs

FINISHING

To close the top of the beanie, thread a tapestry needle and weave through every other row along the edge (**B**). Pull tightly to close.

To reinforce the top closure, use criss-cross stitches (**C**) and pull tightly through to the inside. Tie on the inside to secure (**D**).

Weave in any tail ends.

B

Decoration

A pom-pom will add the finishing touch to your beanie. Using color A and a pom-pom maker, make the pom-pom following the instructions. Use the yarn ends in a tapestry needle to sew it to the top of the beanie.

C

D

HOROSCOPE WRAP

Your horoscope reveals a new clothing piece that can evolve with the changing seasons. This versatile design makes a cute crop top for warmer months, a great layering piece for when it cools down, and can even be worn as a hooded scarf when it's really cold! This customizable wrap is crocheted in the round with a twist, and features all of the Glyph Charts with little star details.

SIZING

Use a non-stretchy string or cotton yarn to measure. You may need assistance if you're measuring on yourself. Start by holding the string end at the center of the chest. Wrap the string around the back of the shoulders, cross over the front of the chest, wrap around the waist across the back, and back up to the center of the chest. Make sure the string is loose fitting and sitting comfortably around the shoulders and waist. Cut the string where the two ends meet. Measure the string and record your measurement.

If you are between sizes I recommend sizing up to accommodate for the bulk of the yarn. For a proper fit, it is very important to check your gauge. To be sure your sizing is correct, crochet a SC row following the chain count below, and use that to wrap around the body, and adjust the size if needed.

Small: 70½in/179cm (10 Glyph Charts) 300 chains

Medium: 77½in/197cm (11 Glyph Charts) 330 chains

Large: 84½in/214.5cm (all 12 Glyph Charts) 360 chains

X-Large: 92in/233.5cm (all 12 Glyph Charts plus 1 extra) 390 chains

For larger sizes, add 7in (18cm), 1 Glyph Chart, and 30 chains per size increase.

YARN USED:

Yardage based on size Large. Add one additional skein of each color for sizes over Large.

Berroco Remix®, recycled fiber blend, worsted 4/aran

- Color A: 4 skeins (about 865yd/790m) Eggplant (purple)

Berroco Vintage®, acrylic/wool blend, worsted 4/aran

- Color B: 2 skeins (about 400yd/366m) Dove (gray)

HOOK USED:

US I/9 (5.5mm)

TOOLS & MATERIALS:

Stitch markers

Tapestry needle

GAUGE:

17 stitches and 17 rows = 4in (10cm)

DIMENSIONS:

10in (25cm) wide, adjustable length

FOUNDATION CHAIN

Begin your Foundation Chain in color A (background color) with the chain count listed for your wrap size (see **Sizing**).

FOUNDATION ROW

Your first round is color A (background), and second round color B (glyph color), as indicated in the numbered column of the charts.

Row 1: Chain 1, and SC into the second chain from the hook. SC to the end.

At this point I recommend using this SC strip to wrap around the body to make sure it's going to fit properly. Adjust the foundation chain count to a different size if needed.

MARK THE ROW WITH STITCH MARKERS

Assign each Glyph a different color stitch marker. You can use the power colors associated with each Zodiac sign, or pick your own colors.

Starting from the right, mark under the first stitch as Pisces, and mark every 30 stitches with the next glyph moving backwards to Aries (**A**).

If you're adding extra symbols, mark those after Aries. If you're removing symbols, you can choose which glyphs to leave out, and only mark the ones you're going to use.

Left-handed crocheters mark from left to right in order from Aries to Pisces.

If you're working with a wrap that's XL or larger you'll have to add additional Glyphs. You can pick a random Glyph(s) for each size increase. Using a random glyph will ensure there won't be two of the same symbols next to each other at the join.

TWIST THEN CONNECT

Straighten the SC row so there are no twists, then carefully twist it 360 degrees so the top of the row is facing up again (**B**). Connect the beginning and end with a stitch marker to hold in place while you join the next color.

Follow the instructions for **Working in the Round From Foundation Row** to join Round 1, switch colors, and add round 2 (all SCs). All remaining rounds will follow the Working in the Round instructions for joining and switching colors.

FOLLOWING THE CHARTS

Each section starts on the left of where the round joins, and all of the glyphs shift to the left by 15 stitches in each section. This means the glyph you used at the end of section 1 and 2 (Aries) will now be the glyph you start with in section 3. If you're adding additional glyphs, the last glyph starts section 3 instead of Aries. Reverse these instructions when crocheting left-handed.

SMALL STAR CHART

13	X	X	X	X	X	X	X	X	X	X	X	X	X	X	X	13
12																12
11	X	X	X	X	X	X	X	X	X	X	X	X	X	X	X	11
10																10
9	X	X	X	X	X	X	X		X	X	X	X	X	X	X	9
8								X								8
7	X	X	X	X	X						X	X	X	X	X	7
6							D̄	\	D̄							6
5	X	X	X	X	X	X		X		X	X	X	X	X	X	5
4																4
3	X	X	X	X	X	X	X	X	X	X	X	X	X	X	X	3
2																2
1	X	X	X	X	X	X	X	X	X	X	X	X	X	X	X	1

Section 1:

Begin following the first Glyph Chart from Row 1 across all 15 stitches. Continue to the Small Star Chart from Row 1 across all 15 stitches. Continue adding the next Glyph Chart followed by the Small Star Chart for the remainder of the round. Follow the charts from Rows 1–13.

Work 1 round all SCs (back loops) in color B.

Section 2:

Move the stitch markers. Mark under the 16th stitch with your first glyph (starting with Pisces and ending with Aries for right-handed crocheters).

Begin following the Small Star Chart from Row 1 across all 15 stitches. Continue to the first Glyph Chart from Row 1 across all 15 stitches. Continue adding the Small Star Chart followed by the next Glyph Chart for the remainder of the round. Follow the charts from Rows 1–13.

Work 1 round all SCs (back loops) in color B.

Section 3:

Move the stitch markers. Mark under the first stitch with your second glyph (starting with Aquarius and ending with Pisces for right-handed crocheters). **If you're using extra glyphs, start marking section 3 with the last symbol used in section 2.**

Begin following the first Glyph Chart from Row 1 across all 15 stitches. Continue to the Small Star Chart from Row 1 across all 15 stitches. Continue adding the next Glyph Chart followed by the Small Star Chart for the remainder of the round. Follow the charts from Rows 1–13.

Finish with 1 round slip stitches in color A.

WEARING THE WRAP

The twist in the wrap helps it to lay flat against the body when worn doubled, but it can be tricky to put it on. Make sure the glyphs are facing right side up and the twist is in front of you. Step into the circle, put the line where the rounds join across your back, and hold it under your arms. Twist the wrap in front of you and place one layer over your head to form the crossed layers effect at the front. Flatten the wrap around the back of your shoulders.

If it's very twisted at this point, take it off over your head and twist it the other way.

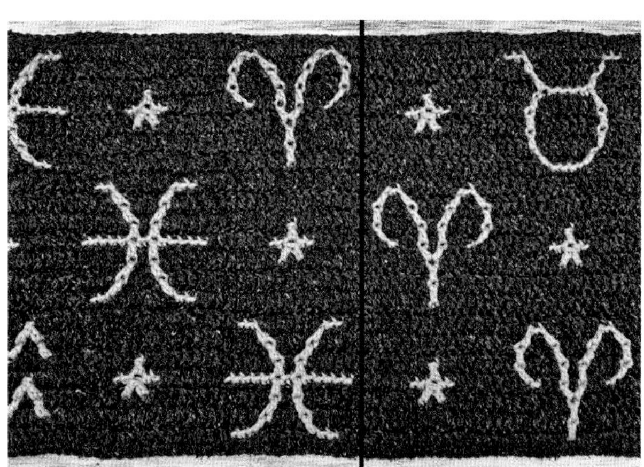

The black line shows where the rounds join

Finished wrap shown flat with twist in the middle

ASTROLOGY WHEEL WALL ART

Create a dreamy, celestial-core wall hanging featuring all 12 glyphs in a wheel, dripping with delicate little crocheted stars. This wall hanging is crocheted from the center out, in the round, and attached to a metal hoop. The center design is the same as the round blanket pattern, but crocheted using thinner yarn and a smaller hook.

YARN USED:

Berroco Tillie™, cotton/cupro blend, light worsted 3/DK

- Color A: 1 skein (about 300yd/275m) Algodao (blue)

Berroco Modern Cotton™, cotton/modal rayon blend, light worsted 3/DK

- Color B: 1 skein (about 300 yd/275m) Coffee Milk (gold)

HOOK USED:

US E/4 (3.5mm)

TOOLS & MATERIALS:

18in (46cm) metal craft hoop

Stitch markers

Tapestry needle

GAUGE:

25 stitches and 25 rows = 4in (10cm)

DIMENSIONS:

18in (46cm) wide, hanging stars about 12in (30.5cm) long

TIPS

It is important to do a gauge swatch (see **Gauge & Sizing**) to ensure a proper fit on the hoop.

For other sizes, make sure your metal hoop is 1–1½in (2.5–4cm) larger than your final crocheted circle.

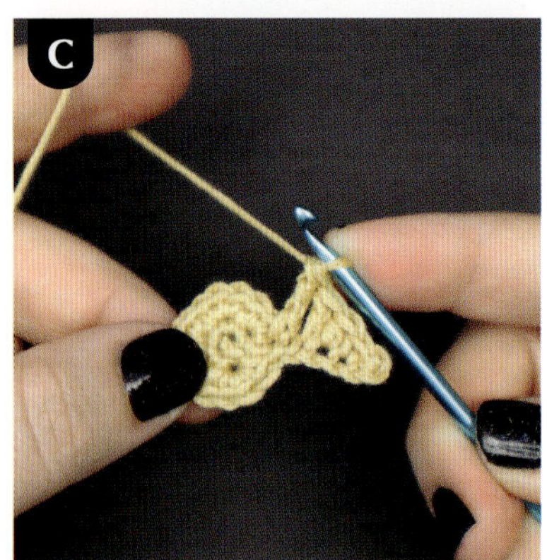

To begin, follow the instructions for the **Astrology Wheel Blanket** from Before You Begin to the end of Round 26A, but ignore the color change in Round 14B.

ATTACHING TO THE HOOP

Create a small ball with remaining color B yarn (**A**). This will help make it easier when wrapping around the hoop. Chain 1, insert hook into both loops of the first stitch, wrap the yarn from behind and over the hoop, slip stitch (**B**). Continue all around the hoop. At the end, fasten off in back.

STARS

Make seven star hangers (three stars on each), and end each with the following chain count:

Four end with 10 chains.

One ends with 20 chains.

Two end with 27 chains.

This will help stagger the stars so they don't overlap.

The stars are crocheted with stitches in both loops.

Round 1: Chain 2, *5 SCs in second chain from hook, join with a slip stitch to first SC.

Round 2: Chain 1, 3 SCs in each SC, join with a slip stitch to first SC (15 SCs).

Round 3: [Chain 5, slip stitch in second chain from hook, SC in next chain, half double crochet in next chain, DC in next chain, treble crochet in base of first SC (**C**). Skip next 2 SC stitches on circle, slip stitch in next SC] 5 times.

Join with a slip stitch to beginning SC.

Chain 17 (**D**).

For the second and third stars, repeat Rounds 1–3 from *, with 17 chains between the stars. After the third star end with 10, 20, and 27 chains instead of 17.

Leave a 12in (30.5cm) tail end for attaching to the hoop, but weave in the tail at the back of the first star.

ADDING A HANGING CHAIN

To add a chain to hang the wall art, leave a 12in (30.5cm) tail and chain 90. Cut a 12in (30.5cm) tail at the end and fasten off. Thread a tapestry needle to the end of the tail and sew at the spoke of Taurus and Gemini, under the hoop, and through the bottom of the chain (**E**). Repeat twice and tie the tail to the back to secure. Repeat for the other end of chain at the spoke of Aquarius and Pisces.

ATTACHING THE STARS

I recommend starching the stars so they lay flat and even. You can soak the stars using a glue and water solution, or use spray starch and steam flat. Be sure to avoid starching the chain in between the stars. Pin the stars onto a mat to fully dry.

Attach the star chains with a tapestry needle as shown in the photo (**E**), in the following end chain count order: 10, 27, 10, 20, 10, 27, 10.

ZODIAC SIGN *Projects*

ZODIAC FAMILY BANNER

Whether you're celebrating a wedding, welcoming a new addition, or representing your besties, a family banner is a great project to honor your loved ones. The banner is crocheted flat with border stitches from the bottom up, and is attached to a dowel at the top and bottom, with extra fringe detail added to the sides.

TIP

I recommend not using more than three zodiac signs to make up a single banner, because adding more signs may cause it to stretch out of shape.

YARN USED:

Berroco Pima 100™, 100% cotton, worsted 4/aran

- Color A: 1 skein (about 100yd/92m) per zodiac sign
    - Cancer: Aloha (teal)
    - Pisces: Hydrangea (blue)
    - Scorpio: Violet (purple)
- Color B: 2 skeins (about 290yd/266m) Black Eyed Susan (black)

HOOK USED:

US H/8 (5mm)

TOOLS & MATERIALS:

Stitch markers

Tapestry needle

Two 12in (30.5cm) dowels, painted black or desired color

GAUGE:

19 stitches and 19 rows = 4in (10cm)

DIMENSIONS:

11 x 33in (28 x 84cm) not including tassels or hanging chain

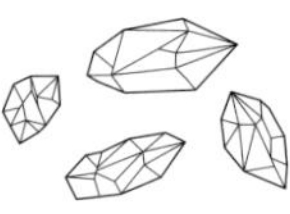

FOUNDATION CHAIN

Begin your Foundation Chain in color A (background color) with 51 chains.

This stitch count includes the 2 border stitches for the beginning and end of the row

FOUNDATION ROW

Your first row is color A (background), and second row color B (zodiac color), as indicated in the numbered column of the charts. Each row alternates between A and B.

To avoid weaving in a lot of tail ends, crochet over all of the color A tail ends (beginning and end of each row) with color B rows (see **Finishing Techniques: Crocheting Over Tail Ends** for full instructions). The tail ends for color B rows will be used to make tassels.

Row 1: Chain 1, and SC into the second chain from the hook. SC the entire row (51 SCs total).

Fasten off and cut a 2–3in (5–7.5cm) tail end.

Row 2: Start with a border stitch, and add SC stitches for the entire row, up to the last stitch. Finish with a border stitch and cut a 3in (7.5cm) tail.

All remaining rows will start and end with a border stitch.

Row 3: All DCs (overlay stitches) color A.

Row 4: All SCs (back loops only) color B.

FOLLOWING THE CHARTS

Choose the Zodiac Chart you would like for the bottom of your banner.

Each row will have 4 blank stitches before and after the Zodiac Chart.

All color A rows will start and end with 4 DCs.

All color B rows will start and end with 4 SCs.

Chart row 1: Begin with 4 DCs. Follow across all 41 stitches on Row 1. Finish with 4 DCs.

Chart row 2: Begin with 4 SCs. Follow across all 41 stitches on Row 2. Finish with 4 SCs.

Continue following the chosen Zodiac Chart from Rows 3–41, repeating the sequence for blank stitches.

Row 42: All SCs (back loops only) color B.

Row 43: All DCs (overlay stitches) color A.

Finish here, or to add a second or third Zodiac Chart, repeat the instructions starting from Row 2. Start Row 3 with your next color.

ADDING FRINGE

Group tail ends into groups of two. For any odd number of tail ends you can add them to the tassel next to it or weave into the back.

Cut strands of yarn 6–7in (15–18cm) long. Insert your hook between the border stitches in the middle of the group of two tail ends (**A**). Add three strands of yarn folded in half to each group of two tail ends. See **Finishing Techniques: Fringe & Tassels** for tassel instructions. Repeat for the other side.

ADDING DOWELS & BORDER

Paint the dowels to match the tassel color.

Tie yarn to both loops of the first border stitch on the top right. (Left-handed: Start on the top left and crochet clockwise around the banner following these same instructions.)

Add SCs into both loops across the top of the banner, wrapping the yarn over the top of the dowel before each stitch (**B**).

Add slip stitches along the border stitches over the tassels (**C**). Repeat for the bottom dowel and last side. Join to first stitch and fasten off to the back.

FINISHING

To add a chain to hang the banner, leave an 18in (46cm) tail and chain 50. Cut an 18in (46cm) tail at the end and fasten off. Thread a tapestry needle to the end of the tail and sew through the corner of the banner under the dowel (**D**), and through the bottom of the chain. Repeat twice and tie the tail to the back to secure. Repeat at the other end of the chain.

Block finished banner and evenly trim tail ends to 2in (5cm) long.

STAR SIGN PILLOWS

Cozy up under the stars with an ultra plush and reversible zodiac pillow. This pillow is crocheted flat with border stitches and features a large zodiac sign of your choice at the center, surrounded by a simple star border. The back of the pillow is a separate panel crocheted in the reverse colors, allowing you to mix and match multiple pillows according to your mood.

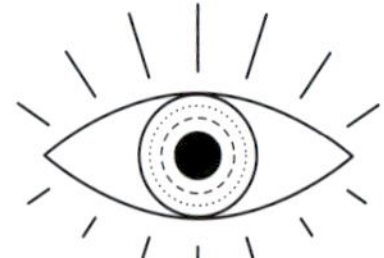

Reverse view

The reverse side of each pillow has the same zodiac sign but in opposite colors, which gives it a completely different look.

YARN USED (FOR ONE PILLOW):

Berroco Wizard™, merino blend, bulky 5/chunky

- Color A: 1 skein (about 260yd/237m)
  Libra: Rhodonite (purples)
  Aquarius: Turquoise (blues)

Berroco Vintage® Chunky, acrylic/wool/nylon blend, bulky 5/chunky

- Color B: 2 skeins (about 260yd/237m) Snow Day (white)

HOOK USED:

US I/9 (5.5mm)

TOOLS & MATERIALS:

Stitch markers

Tapestry needle

Fiberfill, or 14in (35.5cm) square pillow form

GAUGE:

16 stitches and 16 rows = 4in (10cm)

DIMENSIONS:

14 x 14in (35.5 x 35.5cm)

FOUNDATION CHAIN

Begin your Foundation Chain in color A (background color) with 57 chains.

This stitch count includes the 2 border stitches for the beginning and end of the row.

FOUNDATION ROWS

Your first row is color A (background color), and second row is color B (zodiac/star color), as indicated in the numbered column of the charts. Each row alternates between A and B.

Row 1: Chain 1, and SC into the second chain from the hook. SC the entire row. Chain 1, pull down to tighten, cut a 2–3in (5–7.5cm) tail and pull through.

Row 2: Start with a border stitch, and add SC stitches for the entire row, up to the last stitch. Finish with a border stitch and cut a 2–3in (5–7.5cm) tail. All remaining rows will start and end with a border stitch.

FOLLOWING THE CHARTS

Bottom Star Border:

Begin following the Star Border Chart Top/Bottom from Row 1. Follow across all 12 stitches marked in the repeat section (between the bold lines). Repeat those 12 stitches another 3 times for 4 times in total. Follow across the last 7 stitches in the row after the repeat section.

Follow the chart from Rows 1–5.

Row 6: All SCs (in back loops only) in color B.

Zodiac Section:

Begin following the Star Border Chart Left/Right from Row 1. Follow across all 7 stitches.

Begin following the Zodiac Chart of your choice from Row 1. Follow across all 41 stitches.

Follow across the Star Border Chart Left/Right again, all 7 stitches to finish the row.

Follow the charts from Rows 1–41.

Row 42: All SCs (back loops) in color B.

STAR BORDER CHART TOP / BOTTOM

5	X	X	X		X	X	X	X	X	X	X	X	X	X	X		X	X	X	5
4				X												X				4
3	X						X						X						X	3
2			D̄	\	D̄										D̄	\	D̄			2
1	X	X		X		X	X	X	X	X	X	X	X	X		X		X	X	1

Repeat section

STAR BORDER CHART LEFT / RIGHT

41	X	X	X		X	X	X	41
40				X				40
39	X	X	X		X	X	X	39
38				X				38
37	X	X	X		X	X	X	37
36								36
35	X	X	X		X	X	X	35
34				X				34
33	X						X	33
32			D̄	\	D̄			32
31	X	X		X		X	X	31
30								30
29	X	X	X		X	X	X	29
28				X				28
27	X	X	X		X	X	X	27
26				X				26
25	X	X	X		X	X	X	25
24								24
23	X	X	X		X	X	X	23
22				X				22
21	X						X	21
20			D̄	\	D̄			20
19	X	X		X		X	X	19
18								18
17	X	X	X		X	X	X	17
16				X				16
15	X	X	X		X	X	X	15
14				X				14
13	X	X	X		X	X	X	13
12								12
11	X	X	X		X	X	X	11
10				X				10
9	X						X	9
8			D̄	\	D̄			8
7	X	X		X		X	X	7
6								6
5	X	X	X		X	X	X	5
4				X				4
3	X	X	X		X	X	X	3
2				X				2
1	X	X	X		X	X	X	1

Top Star Border:

Repeat the instructions for the Bottom Star Border.

Finish with 1 row SCs (in back loops only) in color A.

Repeat these steps to create a second pillow panel using the reverse colors (color A white, color B purples).

ATTACHING THE PANELS

Line your 2 pillow panels together, right sides facing (**A**), and slip stitch along 3 sides (right, top and left). Place your hook under each of the border stitches on both panels (**B**), and connect with slip stitches along three of the four sides (**C** & **D**). Once you've connected three sides together, flip your pillow case right-side-out and insert your pillow, or stuff with fiberfill. With a tapestry needle whip stitch the bottom closed (**E**). Tie and secure, weave in your tail to the inside of the bottom of the pillow.

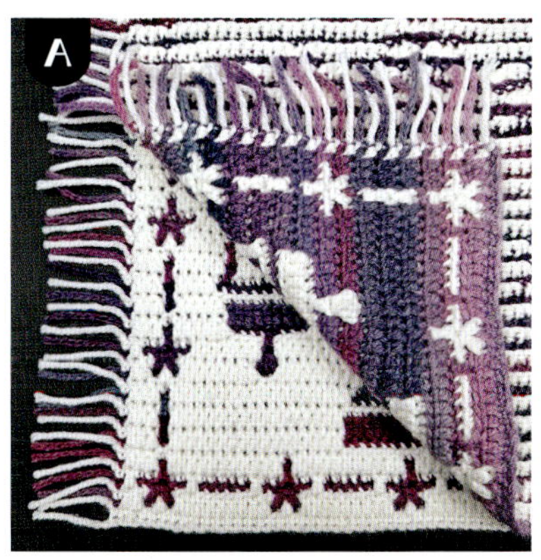

TIP

You can either use a bought pillow pad in the cover, or fill it with fiberfill before sewing up the last side.

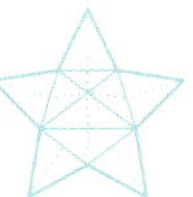

FORTUNE TELLER PLACEMATS

Impress your dinner guests with personalized zodiac placemats. This design is crocheted flat with border stitches, with tassels added to create fringe, eliminating the need to weave in any tail ends. This placemat also makes a great personal altar piece for candles and crystals, or for a fabulous tarot card reading.

YARN USED:

Berroco Modern Cotton™, cotton/modal rayon blend, worsted weight 4/aran

- Color A: 1 skein (about 200yd/182m) Longspur (black)
- Color B: 1 skein (about 180yd/164m) Coffee Milk (gold)

HOOK USED:

US H/8 (5mm)

TOOLS & MATERIALS:

Stitch markers

Tapestry needle

GAUGE:

18 stitches and 18 rows = 4in (10cm)

DIMENSIONS:

Approx. 15 x 12½in (38 x 32cm) not including tassels

FOUNDATION CHAIN

Begin your Foundation Chain in color A (background color) with 69 chains.

This stitch count includes the 2 border stitches for the beginning and end of the row.

FOUNDATION ROWS

Your first row is color A (background color), and second row is color B (Zodiac/Star color), as indicated in the numbered column of the charts. Each row alternates between A and B.

Row 1: Chain 1, and SC into the second chain from the hook. SC the entire row (69 SCs total).

Fasten off and cut a 2–3in (5–7.5cm) tail end.

Row 2: Start with a border stitch, and add SC stitches for the entire row, up to the last stitch. Finish with a border stitch and cut a 2–3in (5–7.5cm) tail. All remaining rows will start and end with a border stitch.

BOTTOM STAR BORDER

Begin following the Star Border Chart Top/Bottom from Row 1. Follow across all 12 stitches in the repeat section (between the bold lines). Repeat those 12 stitches another 4 times, 5 times in total. Follow across the last 7 stitches in the row after the repeat section.

Follow the chart from Rows 1–5.

Row 6: All SCs (back loops) in color B.

ZODIAC SECTION

Begin following the Side Star Chart from Row 1. Follow across all 13 stitches.

Begin following the Zodiac Chart of your choice from Row 1. Follow across all 41 stitches.

Follow across the Side Star Chart again, all 13 stitches to finish the row.

Follow the charts from Rows 1–41.

Row 42: All SCs (back loops) in color B.

TOP STAR BORDER

Repeat the instructions for the Star Border Chart Top/Bottom.

Finish with one row SCs (back loops) in color A.

ADDING FRINGE

Group tail ends into groups of 4. For any odd number of tail ends you can add them to the tassel next to it or weave into the back. Cut strands of yarn in both colors, 6–7in (15–18cm) long. Insert your hook between the border stitches in the middle of the group of 4 tail ends. Add 2 strands of each color folded in half to each group of 4 tail ends (**A**). Repeat for other side to complete the fringed edging (**B**). See **Finishing Techniques: Fringe & Tassels** for detailed tassel instructions.

Block finished placemat on a blocking mat and evenly trim tail ends to 2in (5cm) long.

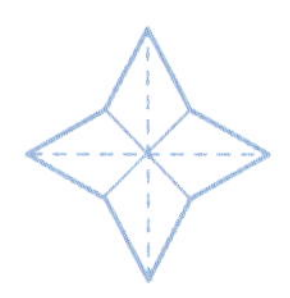

STAR BORDER CHART TOP/BOTTOM

5	X	X	X		X	X	X	X	X	X	X	X	X	X	X		X	X	X	5
4				X												X				4
3	X						X	X	X		X	X	X						X	3
2			$\bar{D}$	\	$\bar{D}$										$\bar{D}$	\	$\bar{D}$			2
1	X	X		X		X	X	X	X	X	X	X	X	X		X		X	X	1

Repeat section (the 12 stitches between the bold lines)

SIDE STAR CHART

41	X	X	X	X	X	X	X	X	X	X	X	X	X	41
40														40
39	X	X	X	X	2	/		\	2	X	X	X	X	39
38						X	X	X						38
37	X	X	X	X	X				X	X	X	X	X	37
36					D̄	D	X	D	D̄					36
35	X												X	35
34		\	2	X	X	X	X	X	X	X	2	/		34
33	X	D	D̄								D̄	D	X	33
32				D̄	D	X	X	X	D	D̄				32
31	X	X	X								X	X	X	31
30				X	2	/		\	2	X				30
29	X	X	X		D̄	D	X	D	D̄		X	X	X	29
28														28
27	X	X	X	X	X	X		X	X	X	X	X	X	27
26														26
25	X	X		X	X	X	X	X	X	X		X	X	25
24														24
23	X	X	X	X	X	X		X	X	X	X	X	X	23
22							X							22
21	X		X	X						X	X		X	21
20						D̄	\	D̄						20
19	X	X	X	X	X		X		X	X	X	X	X	19
18														18
17	X	X		X	X	X	X	X	X	X		X	X	17
16														16
15	X	X	X	X	X	X		X	X	X	X	X	X	15
14														14
13	X	X	X	X	2	/		\	2	X	X	X	X	13
12						X	X	X						12
11	X	X	X	X	X				X	X	X	X	X	11
10					D̄	D	X	D	D̄					10
9	X												X	9
8		\	2	X	X	X	X	X	X	X	2	/		8
7	X	D	D̄								D̄	D	X	7
6				D̄	D	X	X	X	D	D̄				6
5	X	X	X								X	X	X	5
4				X	2	/		\	2	X				4
3	X	X	X		D̄	D	X	D	D̄		X	X	X	3
2														2
1	X	X	X	X	X	X	X	X	X	X	X	X	X	1

TIP

After pulling the tassel strands through the loop add the tail ends on either side to the tassel strands. Then pull all the strands through the loop. See **Finishing Techniques: Fringe & Tassels** for full instructions.

MYSTIC MARKET BAG

This eye-catching yet casual bag is a great size for strolling a local market, or use it as a project bag and stuff it with yarn. The bag features a round starburst design at the bottom, with a large zodiac sign at the center, surrounded by stars. This bucket-style bag is crocheted from the bottom up, in the round from a circle base.

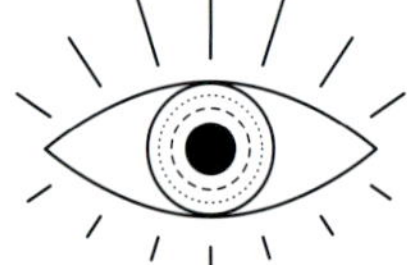

Side view

The side view of the bag features a simple design of large and small stars that complements the zodiac sign on the front and back.

YARN USED:

Berroco Sesame™, wool/acrylic/cotton/nylon blend, worsted weight 4/aran

- Color A: 2 skeins (about 460yd/421m) Ube (variegated)

Berroco Modern Cotton™, cotton/modal rayon blend, worsted weight 4/aran

- Color B: 2 skeins (about 300yd/275m) Bluffs (white)

HOOK USED:

US H/8 (5mm)

TOOLS & MATERIALS:

Stitch markers

Tapestry needle

GAUGE:

19 stitches and 19 rows = 4in (10cm)

DIMENSIONS:

About 15 x 15in (38 x 38cm)

Strap: 2¼in (5.5cm) wide, 28in (71cm) long from top of bag base

To begin, follow the instructions for the **Astrology Wheel Blanket** from Before You Begin to the end of Round 11B.

Round 12A: [1 DC, 71 SCs] twice.

This completes the bottom of the bag (**A**). All remaining rounds will be crocheted in the round with no increases.

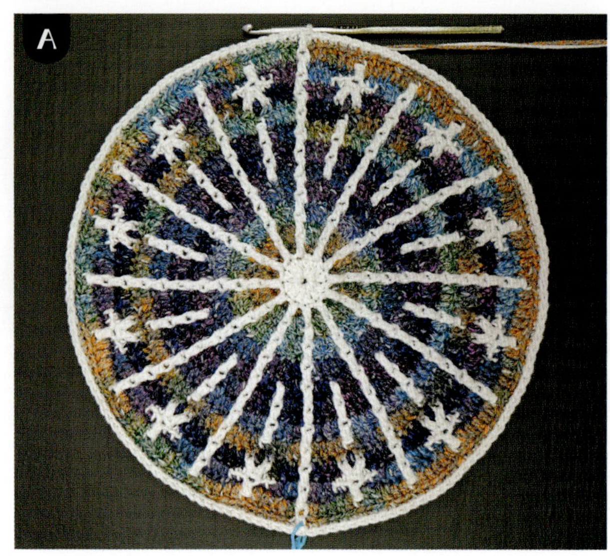

Bottom circle of bag complete

BOTTOM STAR BORDER

Begin following the Bottom Star Chart from Row 1.

Start with the first 9 stitches in the row. Follow across all 12 stitches marked in the repeat section (between the bold lines). Repeat those 12 stitches another 3 times, 4 times in total. Follow across the last 15 stitches in the row after the repeat section. Then repeat this entire sequence once more for the back of the bag.

Follow the chart until you have completed Rows 1–6 for both the front and back of the bag.

ZODIAC/BIG STAR SECTION

Begin with the Left Side Star Chart from Row 1 across all 16 stitches, then follow the Zodiac Chart of your choice from Row 1 across all 41 stitches, then follow the Right Side Star Chart from Row 1 for all 15 stitches. Then repeat this entire sequence once more for the back of the bag.

Continue to follow the Side Star Charts in order for Rows 1–41 for both front and back of the bag.

Add 1 round all SCs (back loops) in color A.

Work 2 rounds all DCs in color B (in the second round crochet in both loops).

BOTTOM STAR BORDER CHART

6	\	2	X			X																								X			X	2	/		6
5	D	D̄		X				X	X	X	X		X	X	X	X	X	X	X	X	X	X	X		X	X	X	X				X		D̄	D		5
4						X						X												X						X						X	4
3	X	X	X	X	X		X	X	X						X	X	X	X	X	X	X						X	X	X		X	X	X	X	X		3
2											D̄	\	D̄										D̄	\	D̄											X	2
1	X	X	X	X	X	X	X	X	X	X		X		X	X	X	X	X	X	X	X	X		X		X	X	X	X	X	X	X	X	X	X		1

Repeat section

LEFT SIDE STAR CHART

41	X	X	X	X	X	X	X	X	X	X	X	X		2	/		41
40															X	X	40
39	X	X		X	X		X	X	X		X	X	X	X			39
38						X								D̄	D	X	38
37	X	X	X						X	X							37
36					D̄	\	D̄				\	2	X	X	X	X	36
35	X	X	X	X		X		X	X	X	D	D̄					35
34													D̄	D	X	X	34
33	X		X	X	X	X	X	X	X		X	X					33
32										X			X	2	/		32
31	X	X	X		X	X	X	X				X		D̄	D		31
30				X						X						X	30
29	X						X	X	X		X	X	X	X	X		29
28			D̄	\	D̄											X	28
27	X	X		X		X	X	X	X	X	X	X	X	X	X		27
26																	26
25	X	X	X	X	X	X	X	X	X	X	X	X		2	/		25
24															X	X	24
23	X	X		X	X		X	X	X		X	X	X	X			23
22						X								D̄	D	X	22
21	X	X	X						X	X							21
20					D̄	\	D̄				\	2	X	X	X	X	20
19	X	X	X	X		X		X	X	X	D	D̄					19
18													D̄	D	X	X	18
17	X		X	X	X	X	X	X	X		X	X					17
16										X			X	2	/		16
15	X	X	X		X	X	X	X				X		D̄	D		15
14				X						X						X	14
13	X						X	X	X		X	X	X	X	X		13
12			D̄	\	D̄											X	12
11	X	X		X		X	X	X	X	X	X	X	X	X	X		11
10																	10
9	X	X	X	X	X	X	X	X	X	X	X	X		2	/		9
8															X	X	8
7	X	X		X	X		X	X	X		X	X	X	X			7
6						X								D̄	D	X	6
5	X	X	X						X	X							5
4					D̄	\	D̄				\	2	X	X	X	X	4
3	X	X	X	X		X		X	X	X	D	D̄					3
2													D̄	D	X	X	2
1	X		X	X	X	X	X	X	X		X	X					1

RIGHT SIDE STAR CHART

41	\	2		X	X	X	X	X	X	X	X	X	X	X	X	41
40	X															40
39		X	X	X	X		X	X	X		X	X		X	X	39
38	D	D̄								X						38
37						X	X						X	X	X	37
36	X	X	X	2	/				D̄	\	D̄					36
35				D̄	D	X	X	X		X		X	X	X	X	35
34	X	D	D̄													34
33				X	X		X	X	X	X	X	X	X		X	33
32	\	2	X			X										32
31	D	D̄		X				X	X	X	X		X	X	X	31
30						X						X				30
29	X	X	X	X	X		X	X	X						X	29
28											D̄	\	D̄			28
27	X	X	X	X	X	X	X	X	X	X		X		X	X	27
26																26
25	\	2		X	X	X	X	X	X	X	X	X	X	X	X	25
24	X															24
23		X	X	X	X		X	X	X		X	X		X	X	23
22	D	D̄								X						22
21						X	X						X	X	X	21
20	X	X	X	2	/				D̄	\	D̄					20
19				D̄	D	X	X	X		X		X	X	X	X	19
18	X	D	D̄													18
17				X	X		X	X	X	X	X	X	X		X	17
16	\	2	X			X										16
15	D	D̄		X				X	X	X	X		X	X	X	15
14						X						X				14
13	X	X	X	X	X		X	X	X						X	13
12											D̄	\	D̄			12
11	X	X	X	X	X	X	X	X	X	X		X		X	X	11
10																10
9	\	2		X	X	X	X	X	X	X	X	X	X	X	X	9
8	X															8
7		X	X	X	X		X	X	X		X	X		X	X	7
6	D	D̄								X						6
5						X	X						X	X	X	5
4	X	X	X	2	/				D̄	\	D̄					4
3				D̄	D	X	X	X		X		X	X	X	X	3
2	X	D	D̄													2
1				X	X		X	X	X	X	X	X	X		X	1

STRAPS

Straps are crocheted from the base of the bag, one on each side, and attached together at the top. From the seam, mark the first stitch in round, count and mark 18th stitch on both sides of marker. Repeat for opposite side of bag, starting from the center stitch on top of the big star (**A**).

Each strap will start with 37 stitches across, and decrease to 10 stitches across.

Work all SC in both loops for straps (color B).

Row 1: Join to first marked stitch, chain 1, 1 SC in same stitch. 37 SCs total, chain 1, turn.

Row 2: Skip first stitch, all SCs to end, chain 1, turn. Each row will decrease by 1 stitch.

Repeat Row 2 another 26 times, until there are 10 stitches across.

Continue adding 10 stitches in each row (do not skip first stitch) until the straight strap is about 7in (18cm) long (or to your desired length.) Fasten off and weave in tail end.

Repeat for other side of strap but leave a 12in (30cm) long tail when you fasten off for sewing to the other side of the strap at the center.

Using a tapestry needle, double stitch through both loops across both straps to connect (**B**). Fasten off and weave in tail.

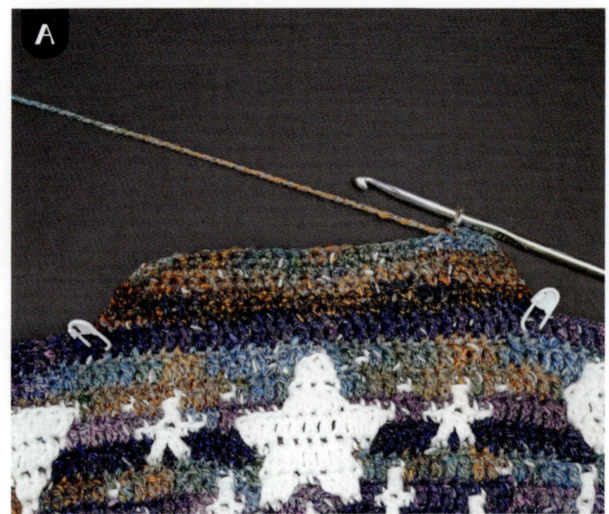

TIP

When using a self-striping or gradient yarn, try to match up the color of the yarn to the last round of the bag when starting the straps. Save any yarn from the skein that doesn't match, so you can use it later to add more length to your strap when the color matches at the end.

FINISHING EDGE

Insert hook into both loops of any stitch along the edge of bag or strap. With color A, place a slip knot on your hook, pull up a loop. Slip stitch in both loops of all stitches around the opening of the bag (**C**). Finish with invisible join. Repeat for other side of strap opening.

INVISIBLE JOIN

Stop adding slip stitches when you have 1 stitch remaining. Cut a 12in (30cm) tail and pull through. Thread tapestry needle and sew through the back of both loops of the first slip stitch (**D**), and through the center of the last slip stitch through the back (**E**). Pull to tighten the stitch to the same size as the other slip stitches. Tie both tail ends together in the back with a square knot.

RETROGRADE SHRUG

Make a bold statement with this retro-style bobble sleeve zodiac shrug. It's crocheted as one rectangular flat panel with border stitches, and is then connected in front of the arms to create sleeves. This design incorporates bobble stitches with mosaic crochet to create amazing texture around a dynamic zodiac sign. The shrug is customizable to fit any size, with instructions for three-quarter length or long sleeves.

SIZING

Three-quarter length sleeves: (about 52in/132cm total length, including cuffs) 229 chains

Long sleeves: (about 56in/142.5cm total length, including cuffs) 253 chains

Record the following measurements before starting your shrug:

Height: Holding your arm out, measure around your upper arm, over your shoulder. Minus 11in (28cm) from measurement = total height of bottom bobble rows.

Opening: Measure from armpit to armpit across your chest.

FUN FACT

In astrology, the term "retrograde" means "moving backwards", so since you're only crocheting this shrug from right to left (or backwards) it's quite an appropriate name! (If you're left-handed I guess you can call it the "Moving Forward Shrug"!).

YARN USED:

Yardage based on 20in (51cm) height, and 52in (132cm) sleeves. Add 1 skein (218yd/100m) of gold for long sleeves.

Berroco Vintage®, acrylic/wool blend, worsted 4/aran

- Color A: 6 skeins (about 1300yd/1189m) Marmalade (gold)
- Color B: 1 skein (about 180yd/165m) Cast Iron (black)

HOOK USED:

US I/9 (5.5mm)

TOOLS & MATERIALS:

Stitch markers

Measuring tape

Tapestry needle

GAUGE:

19 stitches and 19 rows = 4in (10cm)

Note: *It is important to check your gauge after the first SC row to ensure proper fit.*

STITCH RULES

Every row will start and end with color A (background color), and for color B rows in the mosaic section you will switch colors. The color change will be hidden behind DC stitches in the next row.

In order to seamlessly crochet from bobble rows to mosaic crochet rows, all bobble rows are worked following mosaic crochet rules:

- Always crochet from right to left, (or left to right for left-handed crocheters) front side only, (do not turn your work).
- Add border stitches at the beginning and end of each row, and crochet over those tails with the next row. See **Finishing Techniques: Crocheting Over Tail Ends.**
- All SCs for the entire pattern are back loops only.

***Note**: When crocheting over tail ends from the previous rows, the border stitches may become hard to see. Be sure to count all of your stitches to make sure you have a consistent stitch count.*

FOUNDATION CHAIN

Begin your Foundation Chain in color A (background color) and chain the required number for your desired sleeve length. This stitch count includes the 2 border stitches for the beginning and end of the row.

Row 1: Chain 1, and SC into the second chain from the hook. SC the entire row to the end. Fasten off and cut a 2–3in (5–7.5cm) tail end.

Check your gauge at this point to ensure proper fit.

***Note**: In this pattern square brackets are used to indicate a sequence of stitches that is to be repeated.*

BOTTOM BOBBLE SECTION

See **Special Stitches: Bobbles** for how to work the bobbles.

Repeat the following sequence of bobble rows (A, B, C, and D) to your specific height. End with Row D.

Row A: 5 SCs, [Bobble, 11 SC] to last 6 stitches, Bobble, 5 SCs to end.

Row B: 6 SCs, skip chain, [12 SCs, skip chain] to last 5 stitches, 5 SCs to end.

Row C: [11 SCs, Bobble] to last 11 stitches, 11 SCs to end.

Row D: [12 SCs, skip chain] to last 11 stitches, 11 SCs to end.

When crocheting the next row, skip the chain stitch on the bobble (see step 4 of the Bobbles technique).

Completed Bobble sequence Rows A, B, C and D

MOSAIC SECTION

Mark the center stitch. This is the 115th stitch for the three-quarter length sleeves and the 127th stitch for the full-length sleeves.

Now count and mark 20 stitches on each side of the center marker. The Zodiac Chart is 41 stitches from first to last marker. Mark the 15th stitch from right marker (**A**). (15th stitch from left marker for left-handed crocheters.)

Start Row A, continue repeating and stop after last bobble before first marker.

9 SCs, switch colors. With color B, place a slip knot on your hook (**B**), slip stitch, tighten color A.

6 SCs over tails (**C**), cut color A and short tail color B. 41 SCs (chart section), 1 SC, switch colors, 6 SCs over tails, cut color B and short tail color A. 8 SCs, bobble.

Continue Bobble Row A after bobble.

To help keep track of bobble rows and chart rows, follow the key on the right. Each bobble row is assigned to a Zodiac Chart Row.

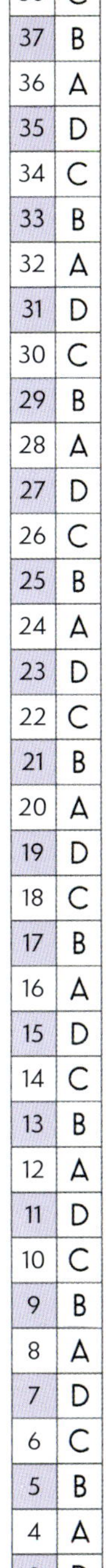

41	B
40	A
39	D
38	C
37	B
36	A
35	D
34	C
33	B
32	A
31	D
30	C
29	B
28	A
27	D
26	C
25	B
24	A
23	D
22	C
21	B
20	A
19	D
18	C
17	B
16	A
15	D
14	C
13	B
12	A
11	D
10	C
9	B
8	A
7	D
6	C
5	B
4	A
3	D
2	C
1	B

Placement of zodiac chart on shrug Purple marker: first stitch in Mosaic Section White markers: Zodiac Chart Stitches (41 total) Black marker: center of shrug

Color B on hook

Bobble row switched to color B. Marker starts chart

First color change row complete

7 DC stitches covering the color change from the previous row

Row 1/Row B complete

ZODIAC CHART/BOBBLE ROWS

Row 1/Row B: Start Row B, continue repeating and stop after last skip chain before chart. 8 SCs, 7 DCs, Row 1 Zodiac Chart, 7 DCs, 9 SCs, skip chain. Continue Bobble Row B after skip.

Row 2/Row C: Start Row C, continue repeating and stop after last bobble before chart. 3 SCs, switch colors, 6 SCs over tails, Row 2 Zodiac Chart, 1 SC, switch colors, 6 SCs over tails, 2 SCs, bobble. Continue Bobble Row C after bobble.

Row 3/Row D: Start Row D, continue repeating and stop after last skip chain before chart. 2 SCs, 7 DCs, Row 3 Zodiac Chart, 7 DCs, 3 SCs, skip chain. Continue Bobble Row D after skip.

Row 4/Row A: Start Row A, continue repeating and stop after last bobble before chart. 9 SCs, switch colors, 6 SCs over tails, Row 4 Zodiac Chart, 1 SC, switch colors, 6 SCs over tails, 8 SCs, bobble. Continue Bobble Row A after bobble.

Continue following the bobble rows with the Zodiac Chart for Rows 5–41.

Shrug flat before closing the sleeves

TOP BOBBLE SECTION

Remove markers.

Continue adding bobble rows all the way across, in this order: Row C, D, A, B.

Repeat 4 times total, add Row C and end with Row D.

Trim any excess tails and weave in any remaining tail ends.

CLOSING THE SLEEVES

Using your opening measurement (armpit to armpit), center your measurement across the top of the last row and mark your first and last stitch.

Fold up the bottom and top of shrug to meet in the middle (**D**). Pin the sleeves closed and try on shrug before stitching closed. Slip stitch through both loops from outside edge to marker, on both sleeves.

ADDING CUFFS

Join yarn at the seam of the sleeve, pull up a loop and chain 2. Add a DC decrease stitch under the first 2 border stitches. (See **Stitches & Techniques: Special Stitches** – these are the DC decrease stitches without any added SC stitches.) Continue adding decrease stitches for each 2 border stitches around the cuff (**E**) and join from back. If you have 1 stitch remaining, add 1 DC in last stitch.

Repeat the decrease round again.

RIBBING

Chain 10. All remaining SCs will be back loop only.

Row 1: Starting in the second chain from hook add 9 SCs. 2 slip stitches in next 2 stitches of cuff. Turn.

Row 2: Skip 2 slip stitches. Add 9 SCs to the SC section. Chain 1, turn.

Row 3: Add 9 SCs. 2 slip stitches in next 2 stitches of sleeve. Turn.

Repeat Rows 2 and 3 around cuff (**F**).

For the last row of ribbing, after last 2 slip stitches, join first and last rows together by adding 9 SCs into the back loop only. Fasten off and weave in ends.

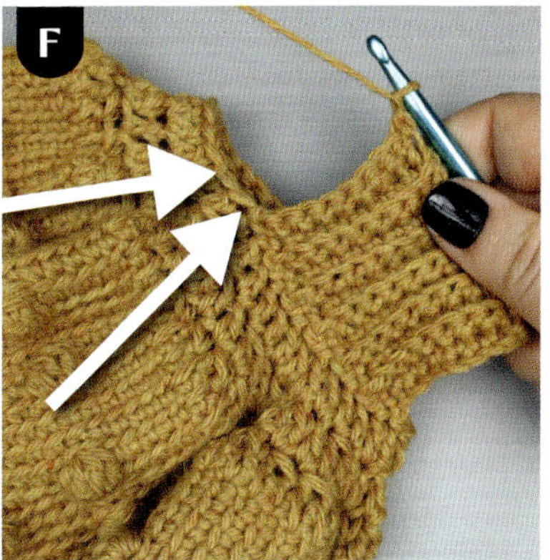

The arrows show placement of the 2 slip stitches on the sleeve

ASTROLOGY WHEEL BLANKET

And now we are ready to put all of the charts together to create an epic twelve-sided zodiac blanket! The blanket is crocheted from the center out, in the round, slowly increasing stitches along the spokes. There are several patterns in this book that follow the same instructions as the blanket up to a certain size.

Get creative

You can also get creative and make other projects like coasters, chargers, pillows, rugs, and more, just by crocheting to your desired size or section.

YARN USED:

Berroco Vintage®, acrylic/wool blend, worsted 4/aran

- Color A (symbols & spokes): 9 skeins (200yds/183m) Snow Day (white)
- Color B (background colors):

Center Circle Section–1 skein (about 95yds/87m) Petunia (dark purple)

Glyph Section–1 skein (about 218yds/200m) Lapis (purple-blue)

Star Cluster Section–1 skein (about 218yds/200m) Blue Moon (blue)

2 skeins (about 250yds/229m) Azure (blue)

Zodiac Section–2 skeins (about 375yds/343m) Tide Pool (navy)

2 skeins (about 405yds/371m) Indigo (dark navy)

3 skeins (about 480yds/439m) Dark Denim (deep navy)

Star Border Section–2 skeins (about 440yds/403m) Cast Iron (black)

HOOK USED:

US H/8 (5mm)

TOOLS & MATERIALS:

Stitch markers

Tapestry needle

GAUGE:

19 stitches and 19 rows = 4in (10cm)

DIMENSIONS:

60in (152.5cm) wide

BEFORE YOU BEGIN

Each round is labeled with A or B, indicating color A or color B used for the round. You can easily keep track of your rounds by counting the color A rounds or color B rounds in the back of the blanket to know which round you're up to.

The instructions in this pattern imply that there's 1 stitch in each stitch, unless labeled as "same stitch", meaning 2 stitches in the same stitch space. The numbers listed as (*#*) are the number of stitches between every spoke. The spokes are the color A lines that divide the 12 zodiac signs. This way you don't have to count all the stitches for an entire round. At the end of each round, join, switch colors, chain 1 (see **Working in the Round: In the Round from a Circle**).

Back of circle showing 6 rounds of color A and 5 rounds of color B

CENTER CIRCLE SECTION

Begin with color A (design color and spokes).

Chain 4, join circle with slip stitch in first chain.

Round 1A: Chain 2, 12 DCs into circle, crocheting over tail (**A**) (12 DCs total).

Round 1B: First color (Petunia for the blanket). 2 SCs in each stitch (**B**) (24 SCs total).

For all remaining rounds, repeat the instructions 12 times.

Round 2A: 1 DC, 2 SCs same stitch (**C**) (36 stitches total).

Round 2B: 1 SC, 2 DCs same stitch (**D**) (36 stitches total).

Round 3A: 1 DC, 2 SCs same stitch, 1 SC (*3*).

Round 3B: 1 SC, 2 DCs same stitch, 1 DC (*3*).

Round 4A: 1 DC, 1 SC, 2 SCs same stitch, 1 SC (*4*).

Round 4B: 1 SC, 1 DC, 2 DCs same stitch, 1 DC (*4*).

Round 5A: 1 DC, 3 SCs, 2 SCs same stitch (*5*).

Round 5B: 1 SC, 2 DCs, 1 SC, 1 DC directly below SC (**E** & **F**), 1 DC (*5*).

Round 6A: 1 DC, 2 SCs same stitch, 1 SC, 1 DC, 1 SC, 2 SCs same stitch (*7*).

Round 6B: 1 SC, 2 DCs same stitch, 1 DC, 1 SC, 1 DC, 2 DCs same stitch (*7*).

Round 7A: 1 DC, 3 SCs, 1 DC, 3 SCs (*7*).

Round 7B: 1 SC, 3 DCs, 1 SC, 3 DCs (*7*).

Round 8A: 1 DC, 2 SCs same stitch, 2 SCs, 1 DC, 2 SCs, 2 SCs same stitch (*9*).

Round 8B: 1 SC, 2 DCs same stitch, 2 DCs, 1 SC, 2 DCs, 2 DCs same stitch (*9*).

Round 9A: 1 DC, 9 SCs (*9*).

Round 9B: 1 SC, 1 DC, Five Point Star Chart Row 1, 1 DC (*9*).

Round 10A: 1 DC, 2 SCs same stitch, Five Point Star Chart Row 2, 2 SCs same stitch (*11*).

Round 10B: 1 SC, 2 DCs same stitch, Five Point Star Chart Row 3, 2 DCs same stitch (*11*).

Round 11A: 1 DC, 2 SCs, Five Point Star Chart Row 4, 2 SCs (*11*).

Round 11B: 1 SC, 2 DCs, Five Point Star Chart Row 5, 2 DCs (*11*).

Round 12A: 1 DC, 2 SCs same stitch 9 SCs, 2 SCs same stitch (*13*).

Round 12B: 1 SC, 2 DCs same stitch, 9 DCs, 2 DCs same stitch (*13*).

Round 13A: 1 DC, 13 SCs (*13*).

Round 13B: All SCs (*13*).

Round 14A: 1 DC, 2 SCs same stitch, [1 DC, 1 SC] 5 times, 1 DC, 2 SCs same stitch (*15*).

Round 14B: Switch to next color (Lapis for the blanket). All SCs (*15*).

FIVE POINT STAR CHART

5	X	X	X		X	X	X	5
4				X				4
3	X						X	3
2			D̄	\	D̄			2
1	X	X		X		X	X	1

Round 15A: 1 DC, 15 SCs (*15*).

Round 15B: 1 SC, 15 DCs (*15*).

Round 16A: 1 DC, 2 SCs same stitch, 13 SCs, 2 SCs same stitch (*17*).

Round 16B: 1 SC, 2 DCs same stitch, 13 DCs, 2 DCs same stitch (*17*).

Round 17A: 1 DC, 17 SCs (*17*).

End of center circle section

GLYPH SECTION

Choose 12 different colored stitch markers or shapes to represent each sign. Moving clockwise from seam, add stitch markers under each spoke section in order from Aries to Pisces (**G**).

When crocheting around, right-handed crocheters will start with Pisces, and left-handed crocheters will start with Aries. Switch to the next glyph after each spoke section.

Round 17B: 1 SC, 1 DC, Glyph Charts Row 1, 1 DC (*17*).

Round 18A: 1 DC, 2 SCs same stitch, Glyph Charts Row 2, 2 SCs same stitch (*19*).

Round 18B: 1 SC, 2 DCs same stitch, Glyph Charts Row 3, 2 DCs same stitch (*19*).

Round 19A: 1 DC, 2 SCs, Glyph Charts Row 4, 2 SCs (*19*).

Round 19B: 1 SC, 2 DCs, Glyph Charts Row 5, 2 DCs (*19*).

Round 20A: 1 DC, 2 SCs same stitch, 1 SC, Glyph Charts Row 6, 1 SC, 2 SCs same stitch (*21*).

Round 20B: 1 SC, 2 DCs same stitch, 1 DC, Glyph Charts Row 7, 1 DC, 2 DCs same stitch (*21*).

Round 21A: 1 DC, 3 SCs, Glyph Charts Row 8, 3 SCs (*21*).

Round 21B: 1 SC, 3 DCs, Glyph Charts Row 9, 3 DCs (*21*).

Round 22A: 1 DC, 2 SCs same stitch, 2 SCs, Glyph Charts Row 10, 2 SCs, 2 SCs same stitch (*23*).

Round 22B: 1 SC, 2 DCs same stitch, 2 DCs, Glyph Charts Row 11, 2 DCs, 2 DCs same stitch (*23*).

Round 23A: 1 DC, 4 SCs, Glyph Charts Row 12, 4 SCs (*23*).

Round 23B: 1 SC, 4 DCs, Glyph Charts Row 13, 4 DCs (*23*).

Round 24A: 1 DC, 2 SCs same stitch, 21 SCs, 2 SCs same stitch (*25*).

Round 24B: 1 SC, 2 DCs same stitch, 21 DC, 2 DCs same stitch (*25*).

Round 25A: 1 DC, 25 SCs (*25*).

Round 25B: All SCs (*25*).

Round 26A: 1 DC, 2 SCs same stitch, [1 DC, 1 SC] 11 times, 1 DC, 2 SCs same stitch (*27*).

End of glyph section

STAR CLUSTER SECTION

Round 26B: Switch to next color (Blue Moon). All SCs (*27*).

Round 27A: 1 DC, 27 SCs (*27*).

Round 27B: 1 SC, 27 DCs (*27*).

Round 28A: 1 DC, 2 SCs same stitch, 25 SCs, 2 SCs same stitch (*29*).

Round 28B: 1 SC, 2 DCs same stitch, Star Cluster Chart Row 1, 2 DCs same stitch (*29*).

Round 29A: 1 DC, 2 SCs, Star Cluster Chart Row 2, 2 SCs (*29*).

Round 29B: 1 SC, 2 DCs, Star Cluster Chart Row 3, 2 DCs (*29*).

Round 30A: 1 DC, 2 SCs same stitch, Star Cluster Chart Row 4, 2 SCs same stitch (*31*).

Round 30B: 1 SC, 2 DCs same stitch, Star Cluster Chart Row 5, 2 DCs same stitch (*31*).

Round 31A: 1 DC, 2 SCs, Star Cluster Chart Row 6, 2 SCs (*31*)

Round 31B: 1 SC, 2 DCs, Star Cluster Chart Row 7, 2 DCs (*31*).

Round 32A: 1 DC, 2 SCs same stitch, Star Cluster Chart Row 8, 2 SCs same stitch (*33*).

Round 32B: 1 SC, 2 DCs same stitch, Star Cluster Chart Row 9, 2 SCs same stitch (*33*).

Round 33A: 1 DC, 2 SCs, Star Cluster Chart Row 10, 2 SCs (*33*).

Round 33B: Switch to next color (Azure). 1 SC, 2 DCs, Star Cluster Chart Row 11, 2 DCs (*33*).

Round 34A: 1 DC, 2 SCs same stitch, Star Cluster Chart Row 12, 2 SCs same stitch (*35*).

Round 34B: 1 SC, 2 DCs same stitch, Star Cluster Chart Row 13, 2 DCs same stitch (*35*).

Round 35A: 1 DC, 2 SCs, Star Cluster Chart Row 14, 2 SCs (*35*).

Round 35B: 1 SC, 2 DCs, Star Cluster Chart Row 15, 2 DCs (*35*).

Round 36A: 1 DC, 2 SCs same stitch, Star Cluster Chart Row 16, 2 SCs same stitch (*37*).

Round 36B: 1 SC, 2 DCs same stitch, Star Cluster Chart Row 17, 2 DCs same stitch (*37*).

Round 37A: 1 DC, 2 SCs, Star Cluster Chart Row 18, 2 SCs (*37*).

Round 37B: 1 SC, 2 DCs, Star Cluster Chart Row 19, 2 DCs (*37*).

Round 38A: 1 DC, 2 SCs same stitch, Star Cluster Chart Row 20, 2 SCs same stitch (*39*).

STAR CLUSTER CHART

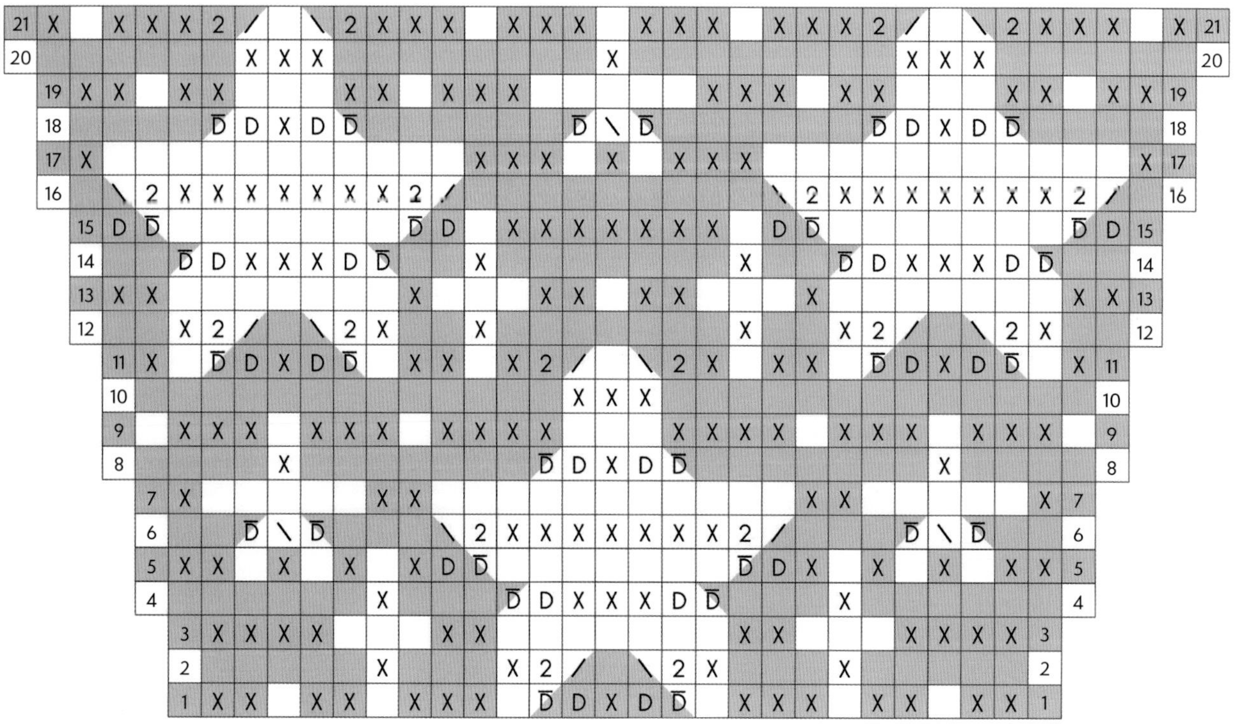

Round 38B: 1 SC, 2 DCs same stitch, Star Cluster Chart Row 21, 2 DCs same stitch (*39*).

Round 39A: 1 DC, 39 SCs (*39*).

Round 39B: 1 SC, 39 DCs (*39*).

Round 40A: 1 DC, 2 SCs same stitch, 37 SCs, 2 SCs same stitch (*41*).

Round 40B: All SCs (*41*).

Round 41A: [1 DC, 1 SC] repeat all around (*41*).

ZODIAC SECTION

Round 41B: Switch to next color (Tide Pool). All SCs (*41*).

Round 42A: 1 DC, 2 SCs same stitch, 39 SCs, 2 SCs same stitch (*43*).

Round 42B: 1 SC, 2 DCs same stitch, 39 DCs, 2 DCs same stitch (*43*).

Round 43A: 1 DC, 43 SCs (*43*).

Move stitch markers up from glyph section to the current round (**H**). Switch to the next Zodiac Chart for each spoke section. (This is to help you keep track of which Zodiac Chart you're working on.)

Round 43B: 1 SC, 1 DC, Zodiac Chart Row 1, 1 DC (*43*).

Round 44A: 1 DC, 2 SCs same stitch, Zodiac Chart Row 2, 2 SCs same stitch (*45*).

Round 44B: 1 SC, 2 DCs same stitch, Zodiac Chart Row 3, 2 DCs same stitch (*45*).

Round 45A: 1 DC, 2 SCs, Zodiac Chart Row 4, 2 SCs (*45*).

Round 45B: 1 SC, 2 DCs, Zodiac Chart Row 5, 2 DCs (*45*).

Round 46A: 1 DC, 2 SCs same stitch, 1 SC, Zodiac Chart Row 6, 1 SC, 2 SCs same stitch (*47*).

Round 46B: 1 SC, 2 DCs same stitch, 1 DC, Zodiac Chart Row 7, 1 DC, 2 DCs same stitch (*47*.)

Round 47A: 1 DC, 3 SCs, Zodiac Chart Row 8, 3 SCs (*47*).

Round 47B: 1 SC, 3 DCs, Zodiac Chart Row 9, 3 DCs (*47*).

Round 48A: 1 DC, 2 SCs same stitch, 2 SCs, Zodiac Chart Row 10, 2 SCs, 2 SCs same stitch (*49*).

Round 48B: 1 SC, 2 DCs same stitch, 2 DCs, Zodiac Chart Row 11, 2 DCs, 2 DCs same stitch (*49*).

Round 49A: 1 DC, 4 SCs, Zodiac Chart Row 12, 4 SCs (*49*).

Round 49B: 1 SC, 4 DCs, Zodiac Chart Row 13, 4 DCs (*49*).

Round 50A: 1 DC, 2 SCs same stitch, 3 SCs, Zodiac Chart Row 14, 3 SCs, 2 SCs same stitch (*51*).

Round 50B: Switch to next color (Indigo). 1 SC, 2 DCs same stitch, 3 DCs, Zodiac Chart Row 15, 3 DCs, 2 DCs same stitch (*51*).

Round 51A: 1 DC, 5 SCs, Zodiac Chart Row 16, 5 SCs (*51*).

Round 51B: 1 SC, 5 DCs, Zodiac Chart Row 17, 5 DCs (*51*).

Round 52A: 1 DC, 2 SCs same stitch, 4 SCs, Zodiac Chart Row 18, 4 SCs, 2 SCs same stitch (*53*).

Round 52B: 1 SC, 2 DCs same stitch, 4 DCs, Zodiac Chart Row 19, 4 DCs, 2 DCs same stitch (*53*).

Round 53A: 1 DC, 6 SCs, Zodiac Chart Row 20, 6 SCs (*53*).

Round 53B: 1 SC, 6 DCs, Zodiac Chart Row 21, 6 DCs (*53*).

Round 54A: 1 DC, 2 SCs same stitch, 5 SCs, Zodiac Chart Row 22, 5 SCs, 2 SCs same stitch (*55*).

Round 54B: 1 SC, 2 DCs same stitch, 5 DCs, Zodiac Chart Row 23, 5 DCs, 2 DCs same stitch (*55*).

Round 55A: 1 DC, 7 SCs, Zodiac Chart Row 24, 7 SCs (*55*).

Round 55B: 1 SC, 7 DCs, Zodiac Chart Row 25, 7 DCs (*55*).

Round 56A: 1 DC, 2 SCs same stitch, 6 SCs, Zodiac Chart Row 26, 6 SCs, 2 SCs same stitch (*57*).

Round 56B: 1 SC, 2 DCs same stitch, 6 DCs, Zodiac Chart Row 27, 6 DCs, 2 DCs same stitch (*57*).

Round 57A: 1 DC, 8 SCs, Zodiac Chart Row 28, 8 SCs (*57*).

Round 57B: 1 SC, 8 DCs, Zodiac Chart Row 29, 8 DCs (*57*).

Round 58A: 1 DC, 2 SCs same stitch, 7 SCs, Zodiac Chart Row 30, 7 SCs, 2 SCs same stitch (*59*).

Round 58B: Switch to next color (Dark Denim), 1 SC, 2 DCs same stitch, 7 DCs, Zodiac Chart Row 31, 7 DCs, 2 DCs same stitch (*59*).

Round 59A: 1 DC, 9 SCs, Zodiac Chart Row 32, 9 SCs (*59*).

Round 59B: 1 SC, 9 DCs, Zodiac Chart Row 33, 9 DCs (*59*).

Round 60A: 1 DC, 2 SCs same stitch, 8 SCs, Zodiac Chart Row 34, 8 SCs, 2 SCs same stitch (*61*).

Round 60B: 1 SC, 2 DCs same stitch, 8 DCs, Zodiac Chart Row 35, 8 DCs, 2 DCs same stitch (*61*).

Round 61A: 1 DC, 10 SCs, Zodiac Chart Row 36, 10 SCs (*61*).

Round 61B: 1 SC, 10 DCs, Zodiac Chart Row 37, 10 DCs (*61*).

Round 62A: 1 DC, 2 SCs same stitch, 9 SCs, Zodiac Chart Row 38, 9 SCs, 2 SCs same stitch (*63*).

Round 62B: 1 SC, 2 DCs same stitch, 9 DCs, Zodiac Chart Row 39, 9 DCs, 2 DCs same stitch (*63*).

Round 63A: 1 DC, 11 SCs, Zodiac Chart Row 40, 11 SCs (*63*).

Round 63B: 1 SC, 11 DCs, Zodiac Chart Row 41, 11 DCs (*63*).

Round 64A: 1 DC, 2 SCs same stitch, 61 SCs, 2 SCs same stitch (*65*).

Round 64B: 1 SC, 2 DCs same stitch, 61 DCs, 2 DCs same stitch (*65*).

Round 65A: 1 DC, 65 SCs (*65*).

Round 65B: All SCs (*65*).

Round 66A: 1 DC, 2 SCs same stitch, [1 DC, 1 SC] 31 times, 1 DC, 2 SCs same stitch (*67*).

STAR BORDER SECTION

Round 66B: Switch to next color (Cast Iron). All SCs (*67*).

Round 67A: 1 DC, 67 SCs (*67*).

Round 67B: 1 SC, 67 DCs (*67*).

Round 68A: 1 DC, 2 SCs same stitch, 65 SCs, 2 SCs same stitch (*69*).

The following rounds will repeat all 7 stitches of the Five Point Star Chart 9 times.

Round 68B: 1 SC, 2 DCs same stitch, 1 DC, [Five Point Star Chart Row 1] 9 times, 1 DC, 2 DCs same stitch (*69*).

Round 69A: 1 DC, 3 SCs, [Five Point Star Chart Row 2] 9 times, 3 SCs (*69*).

Round 69B: 1 SC, 3 DCs, [Five Point Star Chart Row 3] 9 times, 3 DCs (*69*).

Round 70A: 1 DC, 2 SCs same stitch, 2 SCs, [Five Point Star Chart Row 4] 9 times, 2 SCs, 2 SCs same stitch (*71*).

Round 70B: 1 SC, 2 DCs same stitch, 2 DCs, [Five Point Star Chart Row 5] 9 times, 2 DCs, 2 DCs same stitch (*71*).

Round 71A: 1 DC, 71 SCs (*71*).

Round 71B: 1 SC, 71 DCs (*71*).

Round 72A: 1 DC, 2 SCs same stitch, 69 SCs, 2 SCs same stitch (*73*).

Round 72B: All SCs (*73*).

Round 73A: [1 DC, 1 SC] repeat all around (*73*).

Fasten off, secure any color B tail ends together with a square knot and weave in ends. Steam to flatten and even out the center and outside edge.

End of star border section

STITCHES & TECHNIQUES

SPECIAL STITCHES

This section will cover all of the special stitches that create different angles and curves in the charts. This reference guide will walk you step-by-step through each of these stitches so you can learn how to read the symbols in the charts, and see exactly where to place your hook to make them. This section will also cover hidden stitches and special stitch combinations that you'll come across while working through the charts.

Two DCs in the same stitch

A "2" in the chart indicates 2 DCs into the same stitch. Be sure to skip a stitch as indicated in the chart to accommodate for the doubles. (2 stitches will be skipped in the back)

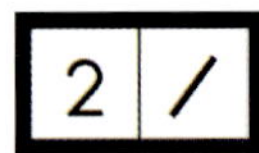

SKIP BEFORE 2 DCS

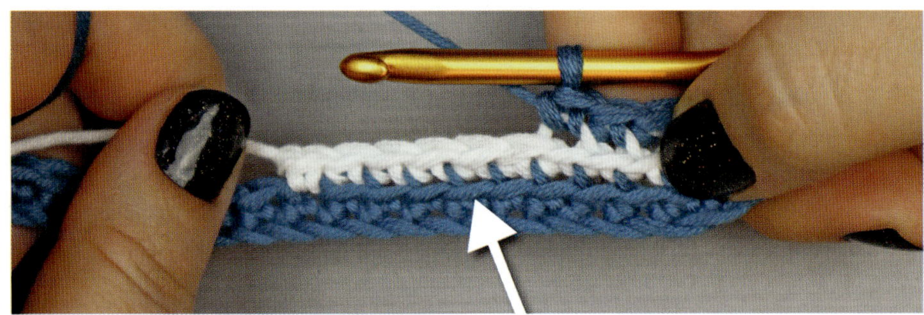

This sequence starts with a skip. Add 2 DCs into the following stitch (as shown by the arrow).

Two DCs in the same stitch after a skip completed.

Left-handed: start with 2 DCs in the next stitch, skip the following stitch.

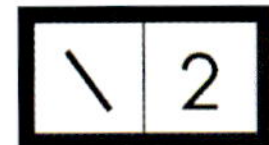

SKIP AFTER 2 DCS

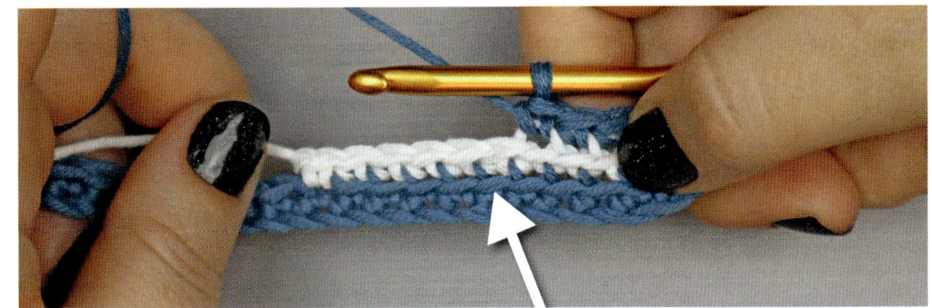

This sequence starts with a 2. Add 2 DCs into the next stitch (as shown by the arrow.

Skip the next stitch. Your next stitch will be in the second stitch (as shown by the arrow.

Two DCs in the same stitch followed by a skip completed. Image shown with 1 SC in the next stitch.

Left-handed: skip the next stitch, add 2 DCs in the following stitch.

Three DCs in the same stitch

A "3" in the chart indicates 3 DCs into the same stitch. Be sure to skip two stitches as indicated in the chart to accommodate for the 3 stitches. (3 stitches will be skipped in the back).

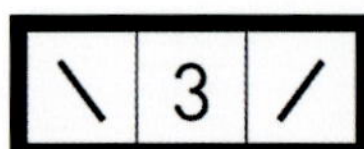

SKIP BEFORE AND AFTER 3 DCS

This sequence starts with a skip. Add 3 DCs into the following stitch (as shown by the arrow).

Skip the next stitch. Start your next stitch in the 2nd stitch (as shown by the arrow).

Three DCs in the same stitch completed. Image shown with 1 SC in the next stitch.

Left-handed: follow the same steps as above.

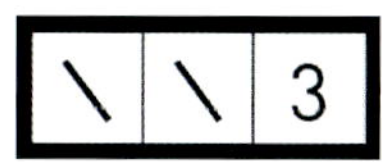

TWO SKIPS AFTER 3 DCS

This sequence starts with a 3. Add 3 DCs into the next stitch.

Skip the next 2 stitches. Your next stitch will be in the third stitch (as shown by the arrow).

Three DCs in the same stitch followed by 2 skips completed. Image shown with 1 SC in the next stitch.

Left-handed: skip the next 2 stitches, add 3 DCs into the third stitch.

3	/	/

TWO SKIPS BEFORE 3 DCS

Skip the next 2 stitches. Add 3 DCs into the 3rd stitch (as shown by the arrow).

Three DCs in the same stitch after 2 skips completed.

Left-handed: add 3 DCs into the next stitch, skip the next 2 stitches.

Diagonals

One stitch will be skipped in the back.

DIAGONAL UP

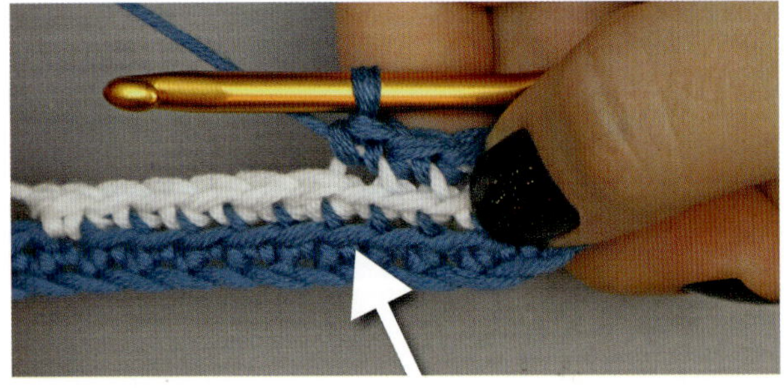

SC in the next stitch. Add a DC directly below the SC stitch (as shown by the arrow).

Skip the next stitch as shown by the arrow.

DIAGONAL UP CONTINUED

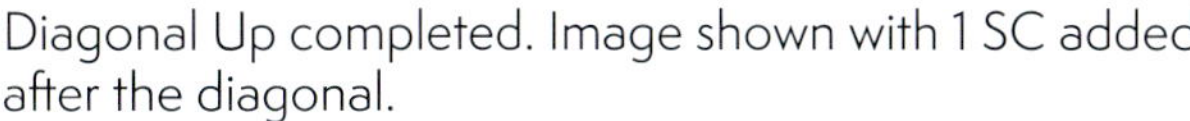

Diagonal Up completed. Image shown with 1 SC added after the diagonal.

Left-handed: skip the next stitch, add a DC, SC directly above the DC.

DIAGONAL DOWN

Skip the next stitch and DC into the following stitch (as shown by the arrow).

Add a SC directly above the DC (as shown by the arrow).

Diagonal Down completed.

Left-handed: start your next stitch with a SC, then a DC directly below it. Skip the next stitch.

Double diagonals

The DCs between skip and SC will make all DCs in this sequence diagonal. They are like diagonal stitches split in half with an extra DC in the middle.

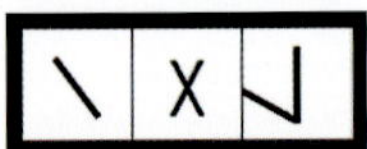

DOUBLE DIAGONAL UP

Start with a SC in the next stitch. Add a DC directly below the SC (as shown by the arrow).

Add a SC directly above the DC (as shown by the arrow).

Skip the next stitch as shown by the arrow.

Double Diagonal Up completed. Image shown with 1 SC added after the skip.

Left-handed: skip next stitch and add a DC into following stitch. Add a DC into next stitch and finish with a SC directly above last DC.

DOUBLE DIAGONAL DOWN

Skip the next stitch. Add a DC into the following stitch (as shown by the arrow).

Add a DC into the next stitch (as shown by the arrow).

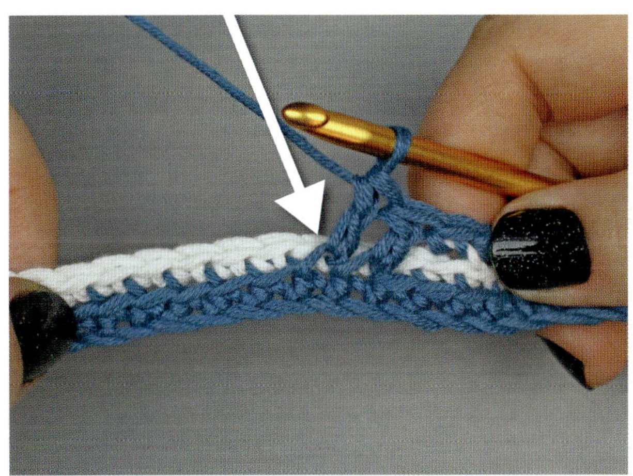

Add a SC directly above the last DC stitch (as shown by the arrow).

Double Diagonal Down completed.

Left-handed: start with a SC, and add a DC directly below. Add a DC into the next stitch. Skip the next stitch.

DC decreases

You'll start with a SC above the first stitch, or end with a SC above the last stitch. All "D"s with a line above represent a SC stitch added above them.

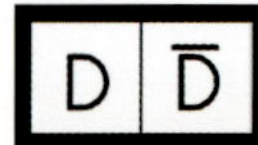

STARTING WITH A SC

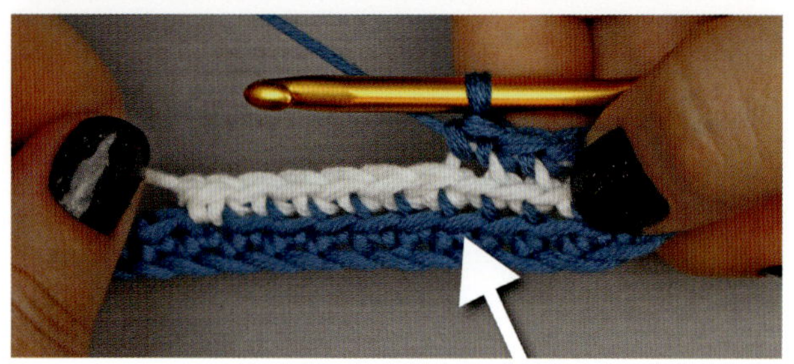

Start with a SC in next stitch. Begin adding a DC stitch directly below the SC (as shown by the arrow).

Work the stitch until you have 2 loops left on your hook. Yarn over and start next DC in next stitch (as shown by the arrow.

Work the DC stitch until 3 loops are left on your hook. Yarn over and pull through all 3 loops. This will connect both DCs into one stitch.

DC Dec Start SC completed.

Left-handed: start a DC in next stitch. Start another DC in following stitch. Finish by pulling through all 3 loops. Add a SC directly above last DC stitch into the next stitch. Skip the next stitch.

D̄ | D

ENDING WITH A SC

Start your DC in next stitch as shown by the arrow, and work the stitch until you have 2 loops left on your hook.

Yarn over and start your next DC in the next stitch (as shown by the arrow), working the stitch until you have 3 loops left on your hook.

Yarn over and pull through all 3 loops. This will connect both DCs into one stitch.

Finish the sequence with a SC added directly above the last DC stitch (as shown by the arrow).

DC Dec End SC completed.

Left-handed: SC in the next stitch and start a DC directly below it. Start a DC in the next stitch. Finish by pulling through all 3 loops.

D̄ \ D̄

DC DECREASE CENTERED

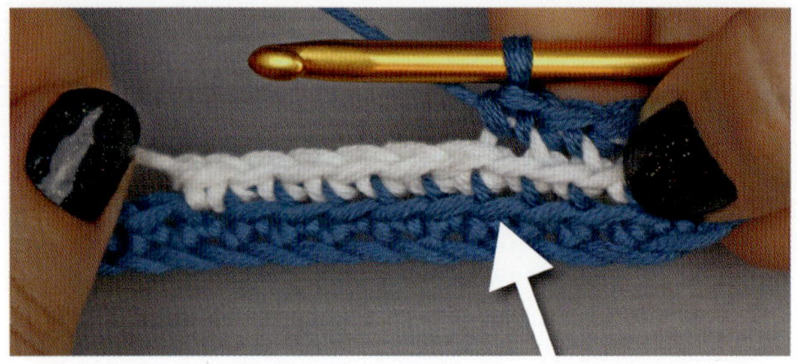

Start with a SC in the next stitch. Begin adding a DC stitch directly below the SC (as shown by the arrow).

Work the stitch until you have 2 loops left on your hook. Skip the next stitch. Yarn over and start your next DC in the following stitch (as shown by the arrow).

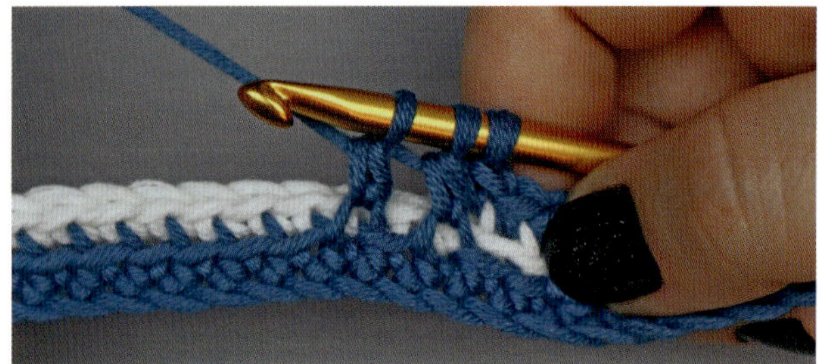

Work the DC stitch until you have 3 loops left on your hook. Yarn over and pull through all 3 loops. This will connect both DCs into one stitch.

Finish the sequence with a SC added directly above the last DC stitch (as shown by the arrow).

DC Decrease Centered completed.

Left-handed: follow the same steps as above.

D̄ D D̄

DC DECREASE 3 TOGETHER

Start with a SC in the next stitch. Begin adding a DC stitch directly below the SC (as shown by the arrow).

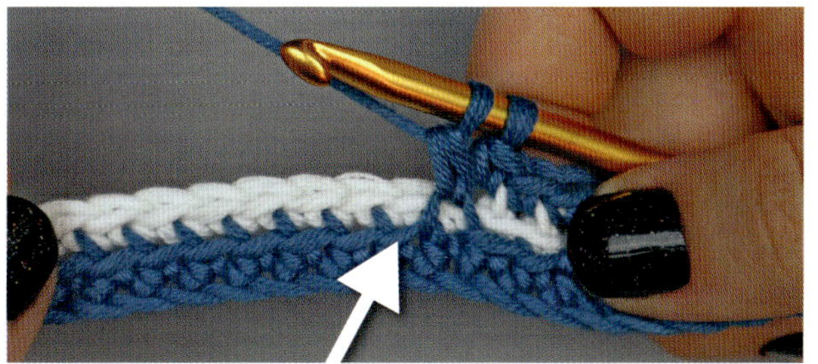

Work the DC stitch until you have 2 loops left on your hook. Yarn over and start your next DC in the next stitch (as shown by the arrow).

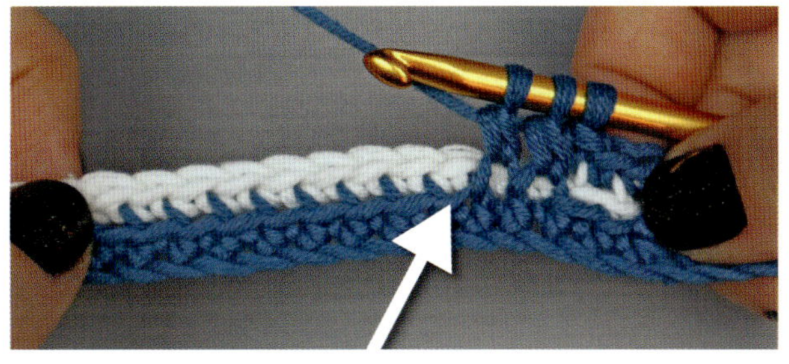

Work the DC stitch until you have 3 loops left on your hook. Yarn over and start your next DC in the next stitch (as shown by the arrow).

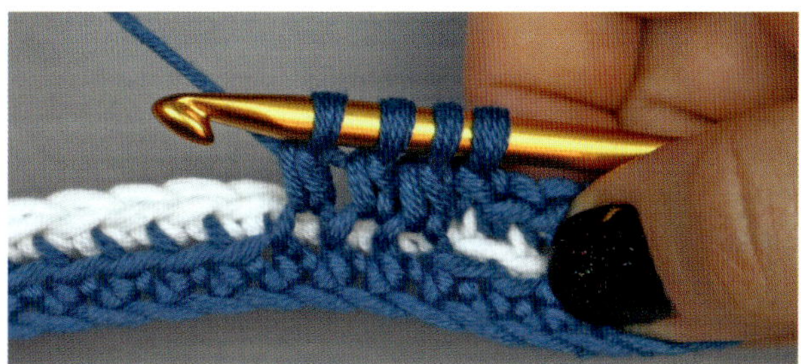

Work the DC stitch until you have 4 loops left on your hook.

Yarn over and pull through all 4 loops. This will connect all three DCs into one stitch. Finish the sequence with a SC added directly above the last DC stitch (as shown by the arrow).

DC Decrease 3 Together completed.

Left-handed: follow the same steps as above.

Triangles

The triangle indicates a DC, with a SC above and a DC below in same stitch.

TRIANGLE

Skip the next stitch. Start with a DC in the next stitch (as shown by the arrow).

Add a SC directly above the DC (as shown by the arrow).

Add another DC back into the base of the first DC (as shown by the arrow).

Skip the next stitch (as shown by the arrow).

Triangle completed. Image shown with 1 SC after the skip.

Left-handed: follow the same steps as above.

Special stitch combos

The special stitches may also be combined in different ways.

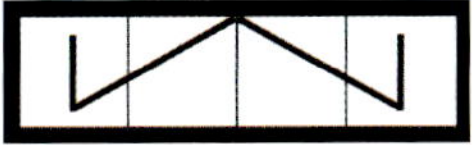

BACK TO BACK DIAGONALS

When a Diagonal Up ends and a Diagonal Down begins, you will have 2 stitches skipped in a row.

$\bar{D}$	D	D	$\bar{D}$

BACK TO BACK DC DECREASE

When you see 4 "D"s in a row, like this, this does not mean 4 DCs are decreased together. These are 2 separate DC Decreases, one after the other. This sequence starts with a SC for the first DC Decrease, then the next DC Decrease ends with a SC.

D	$\bar{D}$	$\bar{D}$	D

DC DECREASES WITH SCs NEXT TO EACH OTHER

When you see 4 "D"s in a row, like this, this does not mean 4 DCs are decreased together. These are 2 separate DC Decreases, one after the other. This sequence starts with a DC Decrease that ends with a SC, and the next DC Decrease starts with a SC, so there will be 2 SC stitches next to each other.

Stacked & Hidden Stitches

When you see stitches that are stacked on top of each other in the chart, this indicates that there is a hidden SC stitch to connect to that is partially covered by a DC Dec or Diagonal stitch. If you push the DC Dec or Diagonal stitch over, you will be able to see the stitch to connect to. Any stitches that are not stacked will be placed into a clearly visible stitch.

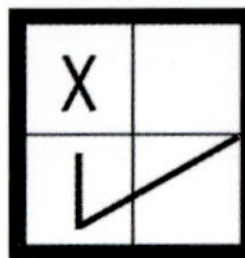

DC OVER DIAGONAL

Hidden SC stitch in a diagonal.

DC into the hidden SC stitch from the diagonal in the row below completed.

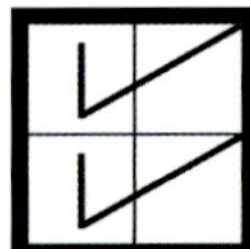

DIAGONAL OVER DIAGONAL

2 diagonal stitches stacked. The second diagonal is added to the hidden stitch from the diagonal in the row below.

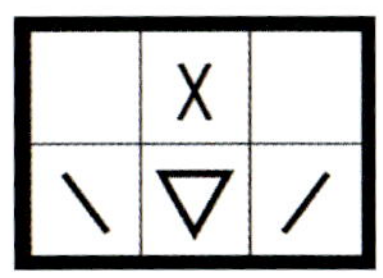

DC OVER TRIANGLE

Hidden center stitch in a triangle.

DC added to hidden stitch in a triangle completed.

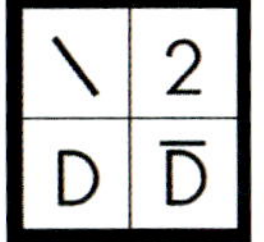

2 DCs OVER DECREASE

Hidden stitch under the SC of a DC Decrease.

2 DCs added to the hidden stitch in the DC Decrease completed. The top of the decrease stitch is skipped.

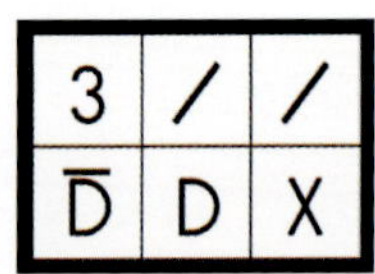

3 DCs OVER DECREASE

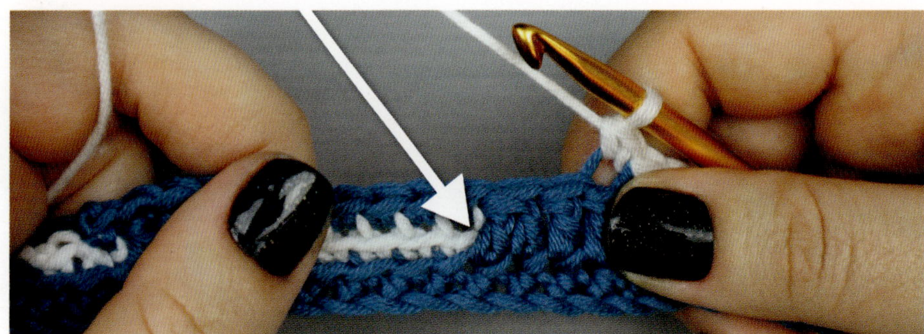

Hidden stitch under the SC of a DC Decrease.

3 DCs added to the hidden stitch in the DC Decrease completed. Two stitches are skipped.

Bobbles

All bobble stitches will be crocheted in the top row, back loops only. Bobble stitches will naturally curve outward towards the back as you crochet them. Be sure to pop all of the bobbles towards you, on the front side of the work.

You'll be working 4 DC decrease stitches in the same stitch to create a bobble.

1. Working into the same stitch, *yarn over, insert hook into next stitch, yarn over, pull up a loop, yarn over, pull through 2 loops; repeat from * 3 more times. Yarn over, pull through all 5 loops. Chain 1. Five loops left on hook before joining bobble stitch.

2. Bobble Stitch completed.

3. Push bobble stitches up from the back as you go.

4. When adding your next bobble row, skip the chain stitch (second stitch) on the bobble. The arrow indicates the stitch to skip.

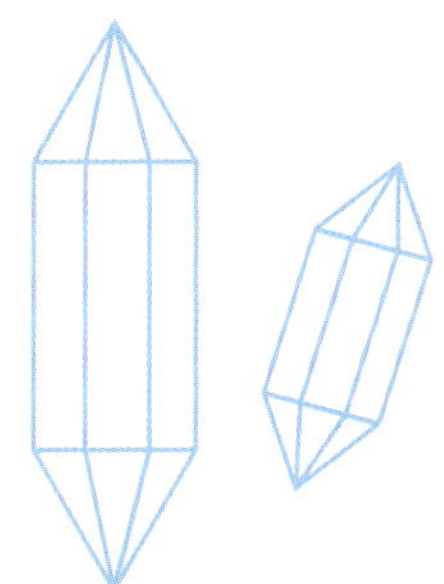

FINISHING TECHNIQUES

CROCHETING OVER TAIL ENDS

Before adding your first border stitch, pull the tail end from the previous row over the top of the border stitch and across the row (**A**). Add your border stitch and crochet over the tail with any SC stitches at the beginning of the row (**B**).

To crochet over a tail at the end of a row, stop crocheting the pattern when you have about 8 stitches (or enough stitches to lock in a tail end) left to the end. Pull the tail back over the top of the row (**C**) and crochet over it with any SC stitches in the pattern to the end of the row. Be careful not to miss the last border stitch (**D**) – it may be hard to see if the tail end is pulled too tightly across the row, so be sure to count your stitches.

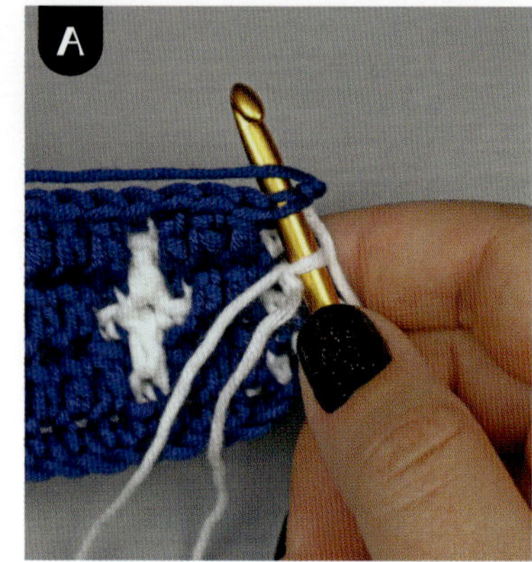

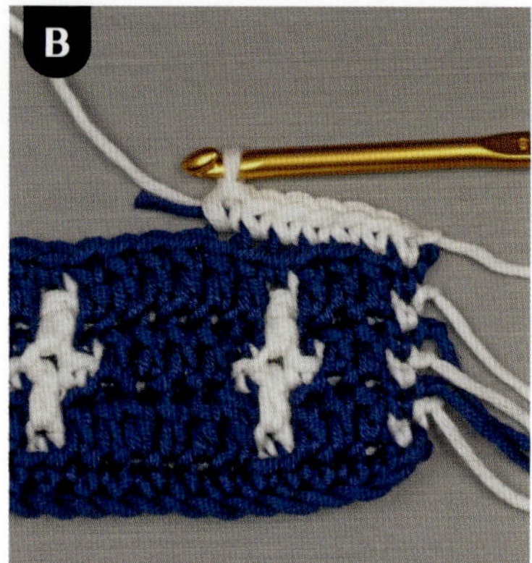

WEAVING IN THE ENDS

The easiest way to weave in short tail ends is by weaving in your needle first. From the back, weave your needle in the same color row as the tail, through about 6 to 8 stitches after the border stitch (**E**). Line up the eye of the needle so it is just above the border stitch.

Now that the eye is right next to the tail end, thread the needle (**F**) and pull through. Carefully trim the excess tail ends in the back.

FRINGE & TASSELS

For quick tassels, wrap the yarn around your hand or other object that's at least 3in (7.5cm) wide, and cut through the loops on one end (**G**).

Separate the tail ends on your project into groups of two or four strands (depending on your pattern). Between the first group, insert your hook from behind and between the border stitches (**H**).

Fold the tassel strands in half (**I**) and pull through a loop. Add the tail ends to the group of tails at the top of the loop (**J**).

Take all the tassel strands and pull them through the loop. Pull the short tails to tighten (**K**).

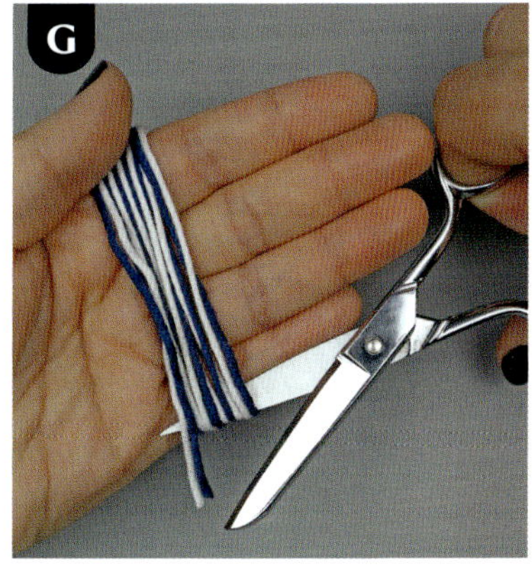

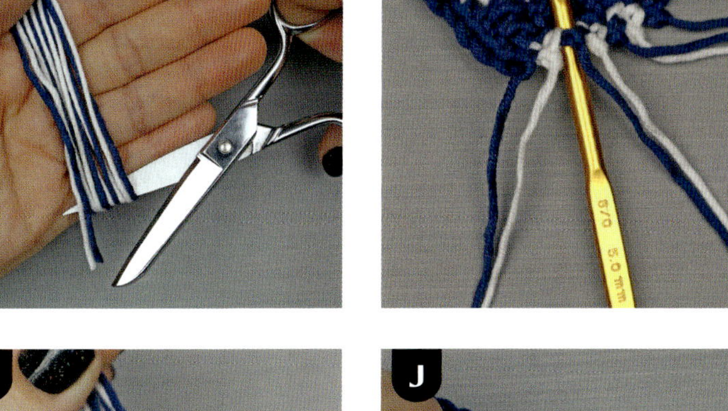

BLOCKING

For flat and straight edges, blocking is key. Mosaics are crocheted from the front side only, and always in the same direction, so this causes your projects to slant on an angle to one side. This may be more visible depending on the type of yarn you're using, but these projects always have a little shift to them. This can be corrected by blocking it on a blocking mat.

Align your project on a foam blocking mat with a grid, using rust-proof pins. You don't want to stretch out your project, just enough to straighten the edges. Use a steamer to relax the stitches, and straighten out any tassels or tail ends. You can also spray your project with water to soak the stitches before blocking it on a mat, and let your project fully dry before unpinning.

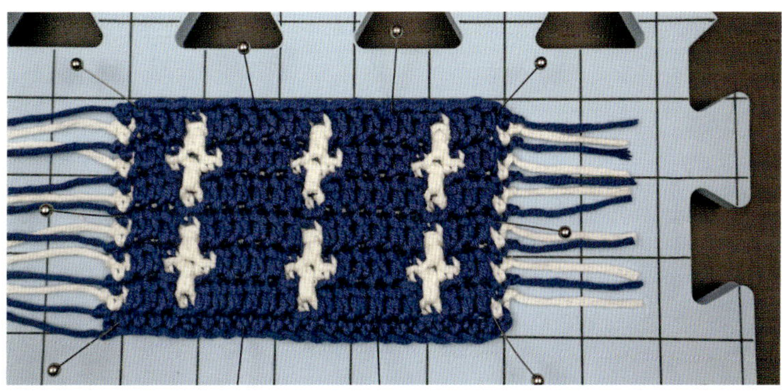

Block crochet on gridded foam mats.

ABOUT THE AUTHOR,

Alexis Sixel, (Aries), is an artist who creates maximalist designs with saturated color, texture, patterns, and drama. Passionate about interior design, modern art, fashion design, and vintage style, she aims to inspire others to broaden their creative horizons. With over 35 years of crochet experience, she's honed her skills to focus on mosaic crochet, and teaching others this exciting technique.

Sixel Design was launched in 2020, and what started as just a hobby has blossomed into an extensive line of unique and edgy mosaic crochet patterns, ranging from Halloween for everyday, to animal prints, geometric designs, florals, and everything in between.

Born and raised in New York, she currently lives in central Maine with her family.

ACKNOWLEDGMENTS

Thank you to the whole dream team at David & Charles Publishing. Writing this book has been such a wonderful experience because of how professional, resourceful, and creative the whole team is!

Thanks to Berroco for supplying all of the beautiful yarn used in this book. Your brand has been a favorite of mine for a long time, so it's been an absolute joy and honor to create a whole book of projects using it.

Thank you to all the pattern testers (The Sixel Secret Society) for all of your hard work. You all provide such great feedback and I couldn't do it without you!

Special thanks to Ginger Hamilton (The Yarn Geek) for being an amazingly supportive friend, and for helping me with all of my zodiac research. And for the endless stream of astrology memes that kept me laughing all year!

Thank you to all my fans and followers! This crochet community is really so kind and supportive of fiber artists, and your continued encouragement and enthusiasm is what keeps me going.

And of course, thank you to my family for putting up with my ultra-Arien personality all these years!

INDEX

A DAVID AND CHARLES BOOK

David and Charles is an imprint of David and Charles, Ltd, Suite A, Tourism House, Pynes Hill, Exeter, EX2 5WS

EU GPSR Authorised Representative:
Logos Europe, 9 rue Nicolas Poussin, 17000, La Rochelle, France
Email: Contact@logoseurope.eu

First published in the UK and USA in 2026

A catalogue record for this book is available from the British Library.

ISBN-13: 9781446315767 paperback
ISBN-13: 9781446315774 EPUB

This book has been printed on paper from approved suppliers and made from pulp from sustainable sources.

Printed in China by Hong Kong Graphics for:
David and Charles, Ltd, Suite A, Tourism House, Pynes Hill, Exeter, EX2 5WS

10 9 8 7 6 5 4 3 2 1

Publishing Director: Ame Verso
Publishing Manager: Jeni Chown
Editor: Jessica Cropper
Project Editor: Marie Clayton
Lead Designer: Sam Staddon
Design: Lucy Ridley and Kirsty Kaye
Pre-press Designer: Susan Reansbury
Art Direction: Sarah Rowntree
Photography: Jason Jenkins and Alexis Sixel
Production Manager: Beverley Richardson

Layout of the digital edition of this book may vary depending on reader hardware and display settings.

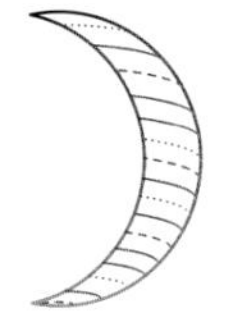 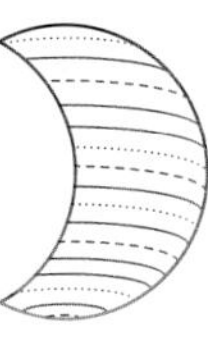 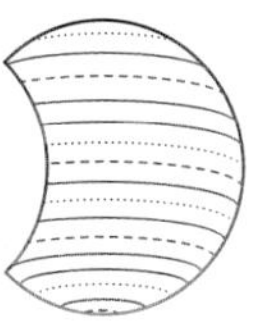   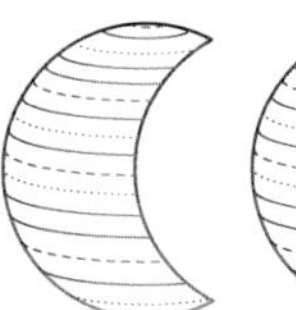 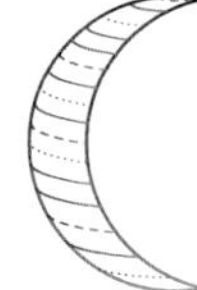